SEVEN WOMEN EXPLORERS

Mignon Rittenhouse

J. B. LIPPINCOTT COMPANY
Philadelphia and New York

Printed in the United States of America by H. Wolff, New York
Library of Congress Catalog Card Number 64-19044
FIRST EDITION

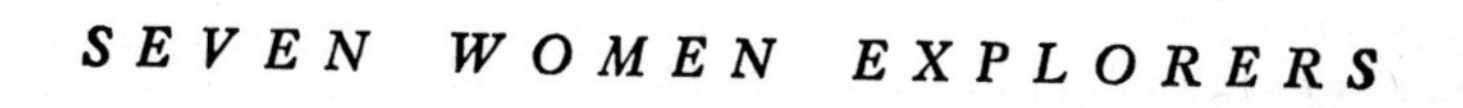

SEVEN WOMEN EXPLORERS

FOREWORD

It may come as a surprise to readers that women as well as men are among the world's outstanding explorers. They appeared rather late in history. There was no such person as a woman explorer in the days of Columbus.

Certainly there seemed to be nothing that would interest a lady in a life dedicated to hardship, loneliness, danger, disease, and suffering, in the endeavor to unlock the secrets of new lands, and very likely leave one's bones to bleach in faraway places. But by the latter half of the nineteenth century, a number of women appeared who were driven by the zeal of the true explorer. Alexine Tinnè, the gently reared Dutch lady, was one of them. She and others were the product of the "new" age of African penetration, the product of Europe's drive to unlock the age-old secrets of the Dark Continent.

In this book are chronicled the stories of seven women explorers of this period, as well as those of the first decades of this century and later. The heyday of these individualistic women seems to have been restricted to a fairly narrow period of modern history. They flourished in America, especially, during the twenties.

The adventures and achievements of the European and American women I have selected, took place in such varied places as the rivers, deserts, and jungles of Africa; the deserts and mountains of Asia; in the Near East, and in the arctic wastes.

The women represent a somewhat restricted field of exploration. Their personalities and experiences are as varied as the locales they traversed. With the exception of Kathleen Kenyon, whose brilliant excavations at Old Jericho put her in the top ranks of archaeological explorers, all of the women in this book—both single and those married to men explorers—had strong urges to blaze new trails in unfamiliar lands. All made more than ordinary contributions to the exploring field.

In this small volume, I have necessarily omitted a great number of "part-time" explorers who made brief sojourns with their husband explorers, but contributed little or nothing to their exploring accomplishments. Such women include Mrs. Richard Burton, and the wives of numerous other explorers—including those of the Norsemen and the wife of Admiral Robert Peary of Arctic fame.

Then, too, there were literally scores of celebrated lady travelers who visited, studied, and made salient sociological observations on foreign lands. I have included one of the best of these—Isabella Bird Bishop. Some contributed important discoveries—others such as the latter-day novelist Edith Wharton who took a brief jaunt into Morocco's harems, were "big names" in search of sensational yarns. Only a few could be considered dedicated explorers in any but the broadest sense of the term.

Since women explorers are fewer in number, and their feats seldom as outstanding, or at least as publicized as those of men explorers, the general public today knows little about most of the women I have included.

In compiling my list, I am grateful for the library facilities furnished by the Explorers Club, the New York Public Library, the Brooklyn Museum, and the Brooklyn Public Library. I am indebted to old scientific journals, old travel magazines and other periodicals, newspapers, and the personal accounts of the explorers themselves, for valuable background information and guidance. I wish to thank, also, the Society of Woman Geographers.

In addition to drawing on these sources, I was fortunate enough to have shared vicariously, as a reporter, in the adventures of such women explorers as Mrs. Delia Akeley, by interviewing her both before and after her one-woman expedition to Africa.

It is to her and to all women explorers whose courage and achievements deserve wider recognition than they have received that I dedicate this book.

Mignon Rittenhouse

Bayside, N. Y.
August, 1964

CONTENTS

SEVEN WOMEN EXPLORERS

ALEXINE TINNÈ

For a woman destined to become one of the most daring of African explorers, Alexine Tinnè's beginning hardly seemed to fit her for the role.

No child ever came into the world with a shinier silver spoon in her mouth than did this winsome blonde baby, Alexine. She was born October 17, 1839, in the court city of The Hague, and was entered in the registry office as Alexandrine Petronella Francina Tinnè. The placid, rosy-cheeked Queen of the Netherlands acted as godmother at her christening.

A life of security and luxury at court stretched ahead for Alexine in a neat pattern as carefully laid out as a Dutch tulip garden. For this beautiful child, there would be the right tutors, the right dancing partners, and, of course, the right husband.

But even in earliest years, there were shades of difference between her and the other stiffly starched children of the noble families she mingled with, hinting of an unconventional destiny. She was far more spirited and imaginative, for one thing. She could run faster, climb higher, had more zest for life. Instinctively, she seemed to be living up to the motto of the Tinnè family—*Aspiro.*

Her father, Philip Frederic Tinnè, was a wealthy Englishman of Huguenot descent. He headed a large Liverpool shipping firm, and for a time had lived in the West Indies. Left a widower with grown children in England, he married the lovely Dutch baroness, Henrietta Marie Louise van Capellan, twenty-four years his junior. He settled down with her in a mansion in the best section of The Hague at 32 Lang Voorhout. From time to time he made long journeys away from home.

His comings and goings became a normal part of Alexine's early childhood, as much so as the regular carriage rides she took with her fashionable mother and widowed aunt, Anna Paulowne, lady-in-waiting to the queen; as much so as the lavish parties given in the candelabra-lighted mansion on each of her father's returns.

Always her tall, graying father came back bearing gifts—delicate silks for a new gown for her mother; a doll in strange Oriental costume or a book with bright pictures of faraway places for Alexine. Once he brought her a pony and cart, promising her a wild horse when she was older. That time they rode together through the shabby sections of town until they reached the lonely dunes. Then they sat in the cart, as waves of the North Sea lashed against the shore. And her father told her of the islands of Shetland he had visited. She listened spellbound. She looked up at him, her golden pigtailed hair framing a radiant childish face.

"Oh Papa, take me with you next time," she pleaded. "I want to see all there is to see in the world."

"Very well, Princess," he told her tenderly. "When you are older, and have learned to curtsy properly to the queen—"

She was barely five when he left on another journey. She waited and waited for his return. She played outdoors less; she clung to the coziness of her back bedroom. Often she perched herself in the window seat, and drew pictures she knew he would like. There was a wild boldness in some, her tutor said; in others warmth and intimacy. One was a water color of the small wooden church the family attended, set in the shadow of the Royal Library. This was the scene Alexine knew best, the scene she saw from her casement window each morning on awakening.

Years later, it was to hang in the English home of her half brother, John Abraham Tinnè, in a heavy-bordered gilt frame. But her father never saw it. One morning, her weeping mother came into her room. As gently as possible, she took little Alexine in her arms and told her that Papa had died on his way to Spa.

So at five, Alexine Tinnè became heiress to the largest fortune in the Netherlands, and the most bereaved of children.

It was her sedate aunt, Anna Paulowne, of all people, who suggested a change of scenery. There was nothing like travel to enlarge the mind and make one forget self, she said. Of course, agreed Alexine's youthful, despondent mother.

At first, their journeys were short ones: hiking in the Swiss Alps, or riding horseback in Italy, then back home to The Hague, where Alexine's training for a debut at court was resumed. For, of course, her mother still hoped that Alexine—with her unusual beauty and artistic talents, as well as the queen's sponsorship—would lead a brilliant social life.

But Alexine, having sampled a foot-loose life away from the restraints of court society, craved more. So at sixteen, she was given permission to travel to Norway, accompanied by a trusted friend of the family, the Norwegian painter, Saae. Through his trained artist's eye, she was shown the wonders of the North Cape. They explored the wild cliffs of the coastline, and saw the glories of the boreal nights.

She returned to The Hague, a tall, slender young lady now, with burnished hair and dazzling blue eyes. In her was a growing rebellion against the artifices of the society around her. She liked nothing better than to astonish her friends and suitors at court by mounting and controlling the fiercest of horses.

But although she became one of the most sought-after girls in The Hague, she was also the most elusive. She had been cautioned often enough to be wary of fortune hunters. In spite of this, she fell deeply in love with a baron, and soon after their engagement was announced, learned he had run up debts, with the prospect of paying them off after his marriage to her. Deeply hurt, she sent him on his way. Now she made comparisons between each new suitor who courted her and the idealistic picture she had made of her father, much to the suitor's disadvantage. More and more, she turned her romantic mind not toward a prospective husband, but toward adventure in far-distant places. By the time she was out of her teens, she had refused a dozen highborn suitors, and traveled with her mother and aunt as far from home as Asia Minor.

In the year 1860, Alexine's imagination began focusing on the puzzling, skull-shaped continent of darkest Africa. This country was calling to many of Alexine's generation.

Half a dozen European countries—particularly England and Germany—were now in a race to unravel Africa's many secrets hidden since the days of the early Pharaohs. They were determined to make accurate maps of this unknown continent, and open up trade routes.

Alexine had grown up on the books of such explorers as the Englishman Mungo Park, discoverer of the Niger River. She knew, too, of the daring feats of such brave men as David Livingstone, Richard Burton, John Speke, Gerhard Rohlfs, and many others.

Her burning enthusiasm to visit Egypt soon rubbed off on her doting mother and aunt, and they agreed to spend a winter with her in semi-barbaric Cairo, in the shadow of the Pyramids. They spent not one winter there, but several. For the first time, Alexine heard the exciting tales of the returning African explorers who had been seeking the sources of the White Nile. Some had been stopped by the falls, rapids, and whirlpools of the river's many tributaries; some by vast wastes of desert and heat; by belts of mangrove thickets and swamps; by savage tribes, hostile slave traders, tigers, lions, and leopards; by dreaded malaria and black fever. Some never returned.

But rather than becoming disheartened by these failures, Alexine went back to Holland only long enough to settle her affairs. In spite of the pleas of friends and of suitors—some of whom followed her to Cairo—she was now turning her back completely on court society. She was determined to give her whole heart to African exploration.

In January, 1862, when little past twenty-two years of age, Alexine Tinnè and her party set out to explore the headwaters of the Nile. In Cairo, she had been warned that it was the worst possible time for an expedition.

There was always deep distrust of white faces in Africa, now more than ever, she was told. Slave hunters had stirred up all the native tribes, far and near, and general war had begun among them. And she was a young, charming white woman, heading an expedition into forbidden regions. She was bringing with her other white women, her mother and her aunt, as well as two Dutch maids.

It was a bizarre group which started from Cairo in three large boats or "*naggars.*" Alexine's "military escort" was made up of Dutchmen and Arabs in Egyptian uniforms, and an Italian interpreter, Signor Conlarine. The rest of her escort were black and brown servants, representing some of the tribes of the Sudan.

Alexine had bought them from slave dealers the year before and freed them, but they refused to leave her. They were only a small number of the large retinue of freed slaves from eighteen Sudan tribes, who now had become her "adopted family" in her Cairo home base. The young ones bore the marks of their tribes. Their bare arms were tattooed with scorpions, serpents, crocodiles, and other fantastic forms.

Alexine had brought provisions enough for a year; ten one-humped camels; her favorite Arabian stallion; and beads of copper coin with which to interest native porters.

In preparation for the dangerous journey, she learned all she could about African languages, customs, and terrain. In Cairo, where she dressed in flowing Arabian gowns whenever she had dealings with the European-hating slave traders, it was rumored that she was the fairest daughter of the Great Turk in Stamboul. This story, she was told by returning explorers, had spread over eastern and northern Africa, and been carried by caravans into the oases of the Sahara. She did nothing to discourage the myth, for she knew it would be helpful to her in dealing with the Mohammedans.

As the three boats neared a bend of the Nile at Korosko, excitement on board increased. Once there, they disembarked, for south of this juncture were many great cataracts of the river. Days of haggling with swarthy caravan leaders followed before she was able to engage a hundred more camels. Then, with only the fuzziest of directions to guide them,

Alexine and her party set out on the weary overland trek southward across the Arabian and Nubian deserts. For seven days they made their way over scorching sand and through dreary gorges, with no fresh supply of water to ease the journey.

When they reached the way station of Abu Hamed, the Nile River once more greeted them. From there, traveling along the eastern bank of the river, Alexine and her following made their slow way to Khartoum, the seat of the government. More than once her mother and aunt wondered out loud what madness made them agree to go with the headstrong Alexine into this world of discomfort and toil. But it was too late now to turn back. Besides, there was a fascination about this journey into the unknown.

At sundown, days later, they arrived on the outskirts of Khartoum. The Arabs in the party prostrated themselves on the ground, giving thanks to Allah for their safe arrival, but Alexine knew that this was only the beginning of their arduous journey. Unless she could cope with the powerful opposition of Musa Pasha, the cruel governor-general who misruled this region, the journey might easily end in the murders of all, here and now.

Khartoum, or "Elephant Trunk," was so named because of the shape of this narrow tongue of land situated at the junction of the Blue and White Niles. Alexine had been told it was a military camp of the Egyptians before becoming the capital of Sudan.

She knew, too, it was the biggest trading center for slaves, gum, and ivory in Sudan. The badly paid Egyptian and Turkish officials, under Musa Pasha, plundered the inhabitants, and with the cooperation of fearful African chieftains, lived mainly by extortion and kidnaping. Bands of Musa's dervishes terrified the region. Slave trade and all its horrors were everywhere apparent. As Alexine and her expedition entered town, they saw miserable, sobbing, captive natives being brought in chains by their black chieftains toward the outskirts, to be sold into lifelong slavery by the cruel Arab and Turkish traders.

Alexine had no intention of submitting her own servants to the tender mercies of Musa Pasha and his gang of cutthroats. She had already made a deadly enemy of him back in Cairo by reporting his traffic in slavery to the Turkish government at Constantinople. She knew he would stop at nothing to keep her and her party from further exploration.

Fortunately, she had the address of Gerhard Rohlfs, the soldier-doctor-explorer, who for some years had made Khartoum his headquarters, passing himself off in these parts as a Mohammedan doctor. After many difficulties, they found his wall-enclosed house, landscaped with exotic palm trees. Though Rohlfs was away on an expedition, they were made comfortable by his Arab servants, and soon visited by other English and German explorers who made the town their base of operation when investigating this region. From these explorers, Alexine learned that there was a higher power in the capital than Musa Pasha. He was the benign Prince Halim, brother of the viceroy, who had proven himself a friend in times past to stranded explorers.

Next morning, Alexine donned an Arabian gown and veil. Then, escorted only by several of her Arab "Egyptian" soldiers, she made her way through filthy narrow streets to the prince's palace.

Her beauty and grace of manner assured her of the protection she sought. She was welcomed as the "Sultan's Daughter," and offered the use of Prince Halim's personal steamer to continue her journey up the White Nile. Elated with her good fortune, Alexine lost no time in getting started.

»»

The weeks passed quickly now. As Alexine, her mother and aunt lounged on deck of the steamer, exclaiming over the tropical scenes of the White Nile about them, the Fashodar country of the Shilluk Negroes came into view. Here the river banks were thickly populated with giant-sized, inquisitive natives, in a setting of mimosa and fan palm trees. Everywhere Alexine looked were groups of wild animals; the colorful zebra and gazelle. And such beautiful birds—the ostrich and secretary! And such battalions of chattering monkeys!

So delighted was Alexine with this section that she decided to encamp here while their steamer returned downstream for new supplies. Though at first her colored attendants refused to land, fearing the wild beasts, giant natives, and especially the slave hunters, they were soon reassured by the reception Alexine received. The story had spread among the natives, and to some of the Mohammedan chiefs on the borders of the river, that Alexine was the "Daughter of the Sultan" and "Princess of the Nile." Her charm and gentleness, as well as her lavish gifts, greatly pleased them. And when she mounted her Arabian stallion with the boldness of an Amazon, the Negroes of this tribe where few white men dared to come, begged her to remain among them. But when the steamboat returned with new supplies, Alexine and her party continued the journey up the river to Lake No, where the Gazelle River empties into the White Nile from the west.

Lake No was little more than a marshy basin, surrounded by stagnant waters with many false outlets and deceptive channels. Many explorers, Alexine knew, had lost their way and their lives here, trying to find a safe exit from its labyrinths. As far as her eye could see, there were endless swamps and morasses, breeding places for typhoid fever, dysentery, and sleeping sickness. Hippopotamuses plunged and snorted in oozing slime. Great birds, ringed by swarms of mosquitoes, stood motionless as statues. On the slimy waters were trunks of rotting trees, masses of moldy water plants and worm-infested floating wood. For a time, her heart failed her. What a dismal forsaken land this was.

As they tried one false passage after another, retracing their course over and over, she dared not show her bafflement. For now her servants were murmuring fearfully among themselves the old legend about the River-God, the Nile, who destroyed all who tried to find his heart. Then, as night began to fall, she caught a glimpse of the White Nile above the lake. They had found the right passage after all—they were safe.

But were they? For next day, when they reached the mission station of the Holy Cross, founded some years earlier by an order of Austrian monks, a cruel welcome met them. Nothing now remained but whitened skeletons, and rows of freshly made graves, mute testimony that this land of malaria and savages had taken its wages. With great sadness of heart, Alexine gave the command to go on to the trading station at Gondokoro, situated five degrees from the equator.

The arrival of an expedition there, especially an expedition led by a white woman, came at an unfortunate time. Always a nest for robbers and nefarious trade in slaves, a Maltese slave trader had only recently raided the tribes of this section. His cruelties had greatly aroused the natives. All this Alexine learned soon after they landed and were placing their stores in the granaries there, before engaging native porters for the overland trek to the south.

No sooner did they start unloading, than angry swarms of savages moved on their steamer. The natives seemed to come from everywhere—from the forests and hills behind the town—from trees, bushes, and the water. No tokens or ornaments and beads could appease them; the answer to friendly overtures was a barrage of poisoned arrows. For the first time, Alexine's soldiers were forced to fire on the natives.

All plans for exploring the region were now abandoned.

Soon, at her command, the steamboat churned up the Nile at full speed. All on board were thankful as Gondokoro faded in the distance. But when they had gone twenty miles, they could go no farther. Gushing cataracts blocked their journey. The health of all had been undermined by the pestilent climate, as well as by trials and dangers met. There was nothing to do but return the long perilous way back to Khartoum.

Since leaving Cairo, they had traveled almost seventeen hundred miles. Alexine had come closer to finding the sources of the White Nile than she dreamed. Yet she felt now that her expedition had ended in failure. If they reached Khartoum alive, she determined she could make new plans based on better knowledge of the country, and try again.

In February, 1863, amid booming of cannon and the waving of flags and handkerchiefs, Alexine Tinnè's second expedition set out from Khartoum.

Prince Halim had made her several months' stay in the town a safe one. Her contact with English, Austrian and German explorers there had greatly increased her knowledge of the country and desire for further explorations.

She resolved that this expedition should be devoted to scientific discovery, so had invited two German explorers, Baron Theodor von Heuglin, well-known ornithologist, and Baron H. Steudner, celebrated botanist and physician, to join the party at her expense.

The two had gone on ahead to distant Meshra to make preliminary arrangements, before the main expedition arrived.

This time, Alexine hoped to explore the Gazelle River, a branch of the White Nile, rising in the unknown land of Niam-Niam in Central Sudan. It was almost wholly unexplored country, and the object of much speculation. Many were beginning to believe that the great lakes in this distant interior were the true sources of the Nile.

Alexine had tried to persuade her mother to remain behind, as her aunt was doing, under Prince Halim's protection. But her mother would not hear of it. Tired as she was of African exploration, she said it was easier to endure hardships with Alexine than to worry about her from a distance.

Alexine and her mother had the use of Prince Halim's steamer again. There were also two passenger and two freight boats, on which were over two hundred soldiers and servants; thirty mules and donkeys, numerous camels, Alexine's horse, and provisions enough for fourteen months. Three thousand pounds of glass beads, as well as twelve thousand ornamental shells and numerous other trinkets were being brought along for winning over the natives.

In spite of the gay send-off, the expedition seemed to be under the black spell of the River-God from the beginning. There was a near mutiny on board the steamer, and after many delays and setbacks they reached Meshra, only to find that more astronomical equipment was needed. The steamer was sent back to Khartoum, while Alexine and her mother remained behind with the main body of the expedition. The small trading post was a place of pestilence—a slimy pool set on a few rods of solid land. Rather than wait in this unhealthy spot for the return of the steamer, Alexine gave the order to set out for the Kosango River, about eighty miles away. But their camels sickened and died under the heavy loads, and the traders they met refused to aid them, regarding them as spies interfering with their internal slave trade. By the time they returned to Meshra, they were greatly discouraged.

While Alexine and her mother stayed at this dreary portage, the two barons penetrated the interior again to seek natives who could aid them in transporting baggage and in further exploration. Almost six weeks passed. Still the men did not return. Alexine waited for them with increasing concern. Then, when Baron von Heuglin returned alone, she knew the

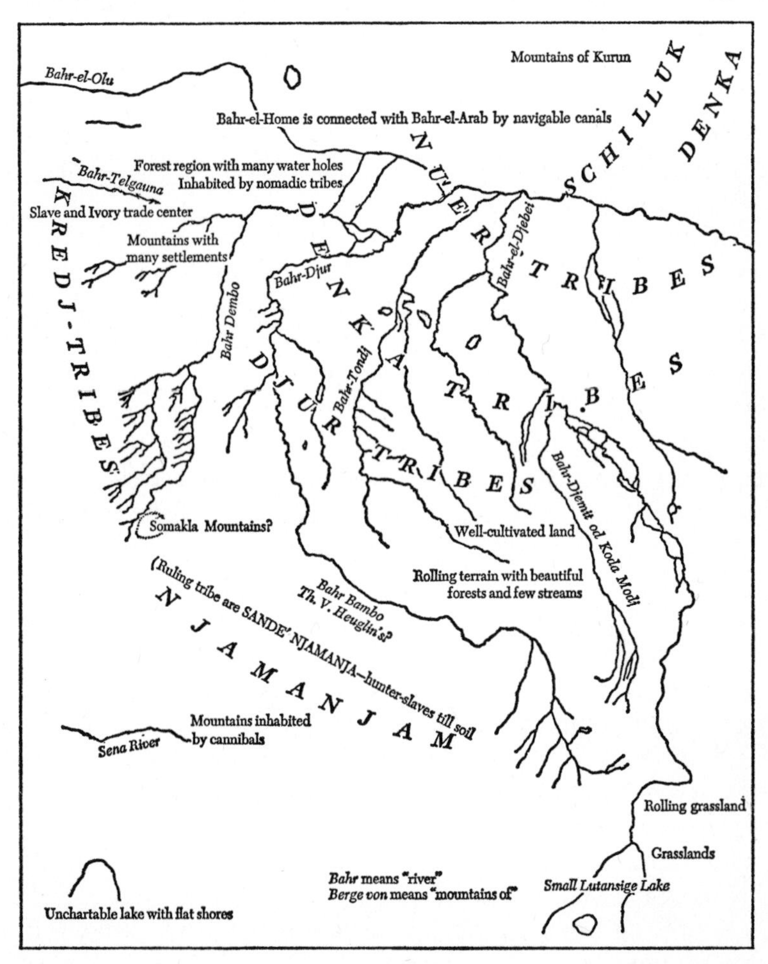

A map based on one prepared by Alexine Tinnè's exploring companion, Baron von Heuglin. It shows the area he and other travelers explored in Central Sudan. Some of the names are in German as the map was published originally in that language.

worst, even before the haggard, sad explorer told her the details. His friend had become ill with fever and died in the wilderness in April. The natives, afraid of leaving their settlements and being seized and carried into captivity, refused aid. As for the trinkets they had brought with them, the country was now flooded with them.

Even the sight of the steamer returning from Khartoum with new supplies, did not lessen the sense of gloom cast over all by the death of Baron Steudner. Because of the long delay the start was made just when the rainy season had arrived, turning the country into one great marsh. Though downhearted, they determined to push forward toward higher ground, secure from the floods. So they made their way across the Bahr Jur and southwest by the Bahr Kosango to Jebel Kosango, on the borders of the Niam-Niam country.

This was not a vainglorious expedition, but a serious effort to chart this unmapped land. In spite of the terrible ordeals suffered on their way—most of their provisions were ruined by constant deluges; their bodies were soaked to the skin day after day; the supplies of the country through which they passed were scant, due to famine—they did push forward.

A missionary meeting Alexine Tinnè and her party at this time told of the compassion she showed to her suffering companions. He told of her placing an ill Sudan "slave girl" on her animal, while she herself waded for long hours through marshes and raging streams.

It was on this precarious journey that she and Baron von Heuglin determined the astronomical position of Meshra-el Rek, the lake whence the Gazelle River takes its rise. Although this lake itself had been discovered by the explorer Lejean, Alexine and her party may have been the first to cross the two great rivers, the Djour and Kosango flowing into the Gazelle River, after traversing marshy regions miles in extent.

This made it possible for them to see where the waters parted between the western upper Nile and two very important streams, the Sena and Makna, which run into the rapid currents of the Benne or Schari. Through this expedition, they obtained important data on a Central African inland sea of great size, situated somewhere under the third degree of the north latitude. This information proved of great help to future explorers.

But Alexine Tinnè's second expedition took a fearful toll. All in the party became ill with dysentery and fever.

Alexine's sweet, gracious mother soon turned into a tormented shadow of herself. She was borne on a litter to higher ground. There Alexine nursed her, but there was no quinine or other medicine to help combat the raging fever. In June, Baroness Tinnè died.

Too ill and dazed to realize fully her loss, Alexine stood over her mother's desert-grave in this hostile Sudan country far from the quaint court city of The Hague.

Then, in quick succession, others died—Baron Heuglin's assistant, the two Dutch maids, the Italian interpreter, and many of Alexine's servants. They, too, were buried in this merciless wilderness.

And when, after delays and dreadful hardships, the remnant of the party reached Khartoum in July, 1864, another blow came to Alexine. For here, too, an epidemic was raging, and Alexine's aunt had died of fever.

Alexine Tinnè returned to Cairo—heartbroken and ill.

More timorous souls would have hurried back to their homeland after these sad experiences. But Alexine Tinnè had an added reason for wanting to remain in Africa—her beloved mother and aunt were buried there. The strange spell this Dark Continent cast on so many explorers, now held her.

Though her half brother, John Abraham Tinnè, hurried

from England when he learned of the family losses, urging Alexine to return to civilization for a time at least, he soon understood that his beautiful half sister had adopted Africa as her own. He stayed on for a time to write a book with her, *Plantae Tinnannae*, which was published in Vienna in 1867. And he made her a gift of a steam yacht, the *Zeemeeuw* or *Seagull*.

In the *Seagull*, manned by a Dutch captain and Dutch sailors, Alexine visited Algeria, Tunisa, Tripoli, and other ports of northern Africa in the next few years. Wherever she went, stories of her generosity and high courage followed her. During the cholera epidemic in Algeria, the "Contesse Olandese," as she was called there, worked as nurse among the sick. Again, in 1867, after a disastrous earthquake, she did much to relieve the poverty and suffering.

It was in Cairo, however, that she was most beloved. She had now become completely Oriental in her dress and tastes. So much so that when she visited the Dutch consul at Tunis in Arabian garb, she was turned away as a Bedouin woman. Yet she would not exchange her dress for that of a European woman, and appeared everywhere now in this fashion, accompanied by a eunuch, as well as by her dark-skinned court.

All in Cairo, especially the donkey-boys (cabmen), of the old section of the town, Massr-Antica, where Alexine lived when in residence, admired her and her fine carriages. They called her, fondly, the "Dutch Countess." They saw nothing wrong, as did her European friends and acquaintances, with her permitting polygamy among her more favored servants, and letting a great colony of pampered, dark women and children grow up about her. During her later travels, it was said her entourage "looked like a band of emigrants on the march."

»»

When an artist friend of hers, Herr Gentz, visited Cairo soon after the death of her mother and aunt, he was guided by the donkey-boys through a maze of narrow winding streets to her home at Massr-Antica; on the way there, he was told many stories of her kindness. On one occasion, they said, she had rescued two poor broken-down donkeys. From that time on, all the sick or worn-out animals were brought to the Dutch Countess to be cured.

She had wanted, they told Herr Gentz, to build a new residence in Arabic style on Nile Island, right near the residence of the rich Ibrahim Pasha. But he would not have this—especially since the Dutch Countess had interfered with his slave traffic, and even asked for his dismissal.

When at last, by tortuous routes, they reached Alexine's residence, the outside of her house looked sadly neglected. But when Herr Gentz passed through dark twisting passages and reached the open forecourt, he found there a well-landscaped garden with three tall palm trees, and above, the bluest of skies. An outside stone staircase led to the back apartments. Here he saw small Negro boys and girls sunning themselves as they played with apes and exotic birds. A tall Sudan woman with flashing eyes and perfect teeth, stared inquisitively out a broken window at him. Then Nubian greyhounds leaped toward him, and an ancient white-headed Berber porter came to greet him.

He was led through a second court and into several museum-like rooms, filled with Alexine's ethnographical collections brought from the African interior. Here were stuffed birds, antlers of a deer from the North Sahara, horns of a rhinoceros, and strangely carved pieces from Niam-Niam.

Soon he was ushered into a gracious sitting room—once a harem—its windows screened with fine latticework, lending mystic charm to the room. The ceiling was paneled in wood, with Turkish carvings; the floor inlaid with marble.

There were many divans, but only one piece of English furniture—a plain wooden table. On this table stood a large Arabian lantern, and several books and sketches of Baron Theodor von Heuglin.

Alexine greeted him wearing an Eastern shawl bound round her fair hair. Her Egyptian robe was of shot-grey silk, and almost covered her mourning skirt. Her feet were encased in Arabian boots of morocco leather.

Although she seemed very sad because of her recent bereavements, her beauty was even more striking than in the past. She spoke with great intelligence and feeling of her life and explorations. She regretted the deaths of her mother and aunt, and felt that her overwhelming urge for exploration had contributed in some ways to hastening their endings, but she could not, nor did she want to change her life. As he sketched several of the young Sudan children and greyhounds flocking around her, she sat—Turkish fashion—on the floor, looking so alive and absorbed in this world she had chosen that he long remembered this scene.

They talked of Gerhard Rohlfs' travels, then being widely discussed in the papers. This former Austrian soldier, who had deserted his regiment, then joined the French Foreign Legion and performed deeds of great bravery, had led a varied, colorful life. For years he had wandered as a doctor to Islam, the Sahara, and later Sudan. Alexine and he had exchanged many letters, she told Gentz—her fair color rising—and she now had in her employ, as steward of her greyhounds, an adventure-struck lad he had recommended. She hoped to make an expedition with Gerhard Rohlfs some day, she said wistfully, for his years of African exploration, in the guise of a Moslem, had given him knowledge and insights rarely obtained by white explorers.

Had Gerhard Rohlfs been able to accompany Alexine Tinnè on her third major African exploration to the unknown regions around Lake Chad, the outcome might have been far different.

He had recently returned to Rome from a Sahara expedition in 1868. Since Alexine planned a new journey from Tripoli to myth-shrouded Timbuktu, she visited Rohlfs by steam yacht for the express purpose of seeking the aid of this great explorer, eight years her senior. The truth is she was drawn to him more than to any man she had met since early girlhood, and with growing maturity, she was tiring of her unrestrained freedom. Much as he wanted to accompany her, he could not go with her at this time, for he had just received a commission from the king of Prussia to accompany an expedition into Abyssinia.

With keen disappointment, and some sadness of heart, Alexine went ahead alone making preparations for her most daring expedition. There was a new element of recklessness, those around her noticed, in her decision not to postpone this journey until such time as Gerhard Rohlfs could go with her.

Late in January, 1869, she set out from Tripoli. She planned to proceed first to Murzuk, the capital of Fezzan; then to go over the Sahara to Bournou and Lake Chad. From there she hoped to accomplish something never before attained by a white explorer—march east through Central Africa, passing Waday, Darfur and Cordafan, to the White Nile.

Her large caravan looked indeed like a band of emigrants on the march as Alexine gave the order: "Forward" in her clear, vibrant voice. She had only brought with her two Dutch soldiers; the rest of her attendants were a large retinue of her pampered Sudan servants. All, Alexine included, wore bright, colorful garments.

The progress of the caravan was slow, and the expedition did not reach the first resting place in Fezzan until March. Gerhard Rohlfs had warned Alexine that this was a place of the fiercest Arabs—the Tauregs, who covered their faces completely, so as to conceal their identity from the authorities and the hapless victims of their plunders. When Alexine in her Arabian garment, was greeted as *Bank-es-Rey*, (the daughter of the king) she felt some of her old assurance. As they bowed and spoke with elaborate politeness, she tried to discount the greed and cunning in their dark flashing eyes. It was the usual thing, she well knew, for these wild Sahara tribesmen to be interested in the baggage brought by explorers, and she had brought more than was customary.

In Murzuk, the oasis city of Fezzan, Alexine felt somewhat weary and ill. While resting, she appealed to Tchenucheu, the chief of the Turkish territory, for permission to enter his domain and spend the summer there until her health was better. She sensed in this handsome, powerful chief, who ruled his subjects and enemies with an iron hand, the protecting cloak she needed to complete her expedition successfully, and she knew beyond doubt that he was sincere when he extended an invitation for her to visit his territory. Since he was about to set out on an expedition of his own against hostile tribesmen, he could not escort her himself. He offered to send a subordinate chief to accompany Alexine on her journey.

Soon after he left, not one, but two hooded chiefs arrived to accompany Alexine and her expedition to Tchenucheu's Turkish country. Each swore to have been sent by Tchenucheu. Each sounded equally convincing. Alexine stared from one hooded face to the other, not daring to make the error of trusting the wrong chieftain. For one, she knew, was a friend of the chief Tchenucheu, sworn to protect her. While the other? . . . With misgivings, she chose the second chieftain.

It was the middle of July when Alexine and her caravan started out with this Taureg chieftain and his band in the direction of Ghat. As they journeyed through this scorching desert wilderness, she felt a little easier in her mind. She was glad there was ample water in the many large containers her servants had bargained for in Tripoli. If the hooded faces around her turned in the direction of these iron containers from time to time, it seemed only natural to her they should be guarding this precious commodity of the desert—water.

To disarm the greed she knew was in the hearts of all Sahara tribesmen, friends or foes, she promised the Taureg chief in imperfect Arabic that lavish gifts would be sent from Tripoli to repay him and his men for safe escort. He seemed to understand her, but she was not certain. His flashing eyes behind the hood seemed to smile approval and understanding.

After several days, they halted at a way station southwest of Murzuk—the Arabs called it Aberjoudj. Alexine and her Dutch soldiers made certain that the containers of water were carefully placed in the largest tent—hers—protected from the fierce Sahara sun.

The night passed quietly. Early next morning, Alexine Tinnè awoke, feeling new confidence that she had chosen the right chieftain. She heard his hearty voice outside, shouting directions to the camel drivers who were reloading the animals in preparation for resuming the journey.

Soon her two armed Dutch soldiers brought breakfast rations to her tent, and stayed to chat with her a few minutes, setting their firearms on top of one of the iron containers. They spoke in heavy Dutch accent, bringing back nostalgic memories to Alexine of her homeland. Perhaps—after this adventure—she would be ready to return. Perhaps—

As the two men were about to leave, fierce Arabic oaths outside the tent assailed their ears. Obviously, the camel drivers were quarreling again, but then, camel drivers were always quarreling. In their haste to stop the quarrel and get on with the journey, Alexine Tinnè and her Dutch soldiers hurried outside—unarmed. As they did so, the Taureg chieftain stepped swiftly behind Alexine and entered her tent.

In stunned surprise, she turned around. Now she saw the flash of his lance, and no hint of friendliness in his crafty, half-concealed eyes—only burning hatred for the white Europeans, and lust for riches. In a sickening moment, she understood. He was not her protector and a friend of the chief Tchenucheu, but the cruel leader of a robber band! And he believed the containers were filled, not with water, but with valuables and money! Now she regretted having guarded them so carefully. If only she could make him understand—if only she could appeal to his mercy—

But there was no mercy in him, she knew now beyond all doubt! His arm rose. As he gripped his dazzling lance, she cried out. Swiftly the lance struck her. A lightning-like thrust, and with it, she felt a sharp stab of pain. She staggered, falling to the ground. Dimly she heard a shot from outside the tent, even as a protective numbness came over her.

She did not see the Dutch soldiers wheel about as they heard her screams. She did not see them kneel beside her to stem the flow of blood gushing from her dismembered arm. She did not see them fall—murdered unmercifully, too, by shot and by lance.

Nor did she live to see the bloodthirsty Tauregs fall on the iron water containers in her tent. Then, disillusioned at discovering no treasures of money and valuables, only water, they turned in rage on her faithful Negro servants, slaying some, and seizing others to carry off into slavery.

Not until September 20, 1869, did news come from Tripoli—and spread throughout western Europe—of the awful tragedy which had overtaken the beautiful Alexine Tinnè and her expedition at a lonely way station of the Sahara desert.

Tearful, frightened Sudan servants of hers—those few who had not been killed or taken away in chains by the wild Tauregs—brought back the terrible story.

In time, with the aid of Tchenucheu, the Taureg assassins

were seized and punished by the Turkish magistrates, and part of the caravan equipment recovered. Only one of Alexine's many Sudan servants—a young woman called Jasminia—had betrayed her mistress's faith. She protested, trembling, that she had been forced to join the robber band.

On October 19, 1873, in The Hague, an imposing brick church was dedicated to St. John and St. Philip. It was donated by the wealthy John Abraham Tinnè in memory of his lovely half sister, Alexine Tinnè, murdered in August, 1869, by wild Sahara tribesmen.

The new church replaced the small Anglican church to which the family belonged—the wooden church in the shadow of the Royal Library, once sketched and water colored by the child Alexine, as she sat perched on a window seat in the back bedroom of the mansion where she had been born.

As bells tolled, and celebrated persons from all parts of the continent quietly entered the new church for services, some recalled sadly Alexine Tinnè's untimely death, before she was thirty years of age. But others remembered with pride the highlights in the life of this fascinating woman explorer, whose pioneering in Africa would light the way for those who came after her.

FLORENCE VON SASS BAKER

"The pilgrim's wife followed him weary and footsore through all his difficulties, led, not by choice, but by devotion, and in times of misery and sickness her tender care saved his life and prospered the expedition."

So did the English explorer, Samuel White Baker, tell of the important role his Hungarian wife, Florence von Sass Baker, played in their African explorations. However, since the perils they faced were mutual, and the youthful Florence was a tenderfoot of tenderfoots when they began their exciting journeys together in 1861, Samuel Baker was called upon quite often not only to save her life as well as his own, but to act as knight gallant to his charming companion.

When the honor of his "lady faire" was threatened, he liked nothing better than to challenge some despotic native king by whipping out his pistol, or warding off enemies by hoisting the Union Jack in awe-inspiring ceremonies.

It was Baker who later suggested that English missionaries be sent to Africa, clad not in dour black robes, which brought out superstitious fears in the natives, but wearing Highland kilts, and blowing lively tunes on their bagpipes. He knew from experience what devices won their aid, at least for the moment.

Only a David Livingstone, with the clear voice of truth speaking through him, and the single eye of the healer, could walk among the natives in ordinary dress at this time, with neither flag nor trumpets to embellish his message. And even he held hostile tribes in obedience on occasion by whipping out his pistol.

To Florence von Sass Baker, the stocky, middle-aged Samuel Baker, with heavy beard and dark as an Arab, was the prince for whom she had waited all during her sheltered childhood. He never failed her.

The saga of this loving couple who conquered darkest Africa together, who won honors and the titles of Sir and Lady Baker, stands out in happy contrast to that of the tragic Dutch heiress, Alexine Tinnè. In contrast, too, to the career of the turbulent African explorer, Richard Burton, who usually left his wife Isabel behind in England when he set off on his many journeys. Yet Samuel Baker did his best to persuade Florence to remain behind with her family when, after their marriage in 1860, he proposed going at his own expense to trace the sources of the White Nile and find his lost friend and fellow explorer, Captain John Hanning Speke.

Born in London in 1821, the son of a West India merchant, Samuel Baker was educated as an engineer in both England and Germany. When he married the much younger Florence on the continent, he was a widower and seasoned traveler. He had superintended the building of the first railway in Turkey connecting the Danube and Black Sea. For eight years he had been in Ceylon, elephant hunting, and cutting down forests and jungles in order to establish an English colony there.

The petite Florence—with shining blonde hair braided in crown effect around her head, and dimpled chin—listened eagerly as he told of past adventures. Then, shortly after their honeymoon, she blithely announced that from now on, she was tagging along with him on his future explorations. There was nothing he could do to stop her, even though he painted as dismal a picture as possible of Africa and its perils.

That is how it happened that on February 15, 1863, Florence and Samuel were "entertaining" under the sheltering awning on the deck of their iron boat. The boat was anchored in the Nile along with several others at the wretched way station of Gondokoro. The couple were playing hostess and host to two long-lost Englishmen.

For two years, the Bakers had been in Africa, exploring the Abyssian border around the Atbara and other Nile tributaries, hunting elephants, and learning Arabic. Wherever they went, they made inquiries about John Speke and his companion, J. A. Grant, who had been sent out by the Royal Geographical Society of England several years before.

Until they reached Gondokoro, there were no clues as to the explorers' whereabouts. Then natives told them that two Englishmen with "wondrous firearms" had been captured by a hostile chief far in the interior, and one of them slain.

Now, when they had given up hope of finding Speke and Grant alive or dead, the two emaciated, travel-worn Englishmen wandered into the Baker camp at Gondokoro.

Later, refreshed and bathed, they sat on deck of the Baker boat, while Florence—in a demure pink muslin gown that showed off her golden tan—served them a tinned ham and brandy from "dear old England." And in this hospitable setting, Speke told them a fantastic tale.

With their own eyes, declared John Speke, *he and Captain Grant had seen the White Nile gushing forth from one of three inland lakes in Central Africa, a lake Speke had reached alone on a previous expedition, and named Victoria Nyanza. He and Grant had satisfied themselves that the Nile flowed from the north end of that lake by way of Ripon Falls.*

Then Speke brought out crudely drawn maps and astronomical findings to back up the remarkable claim. As Florence and Samuel gazed at the region of Central Africa around Lake Tanganyika and Victoria Nyanza, with the fabulous "mountains of the moon" Speke had sketched in as background, they were by turns incredulous, overwhelmed, and disappointed. For in their hearts they hoped, as had so many other explorers, to find the sources of the White Nile themselves—those mysterious, life-giving sources hidden from civilized mankind for over two thousand years.

Finally Samuel Baker leaned back in his deck chair, lit a pipe, and congratulated John Speke and James Grant for their great achievement. But Speke replied:

"A leaf yet remains on the laurel. Why not carry on for us and for England when we return home? There is another great body of water farther north which the natives told us connects with this lake. Because of wretched health and tribal uprisings, we were unable to explore it. But you, my dear Baker—"

"I'll find it!" Baker cried eagerly.

"*We'll* find it," said Florence with gentle insistence.

Speke eyed the small gray-eyed woman—scarcely more than a girl—with sudden misgivings.

"The journey to the lakes is far too dangerous for a white woman to make—especially a pretty white woman—"

"I'll dress as a lad," laughed Florence, the dimple in her chin deepening.

Late in February, 1863, Speke and Grant left for England, giving minute instructions for reaching the Central Africa lake country. In March, Florence and Samuel set off on horseback southward for the garrison of Faloro, the first lap of their long journey.

Their caravan included twenty-nine camels and twenty-one donkeys burdened with luggage, beads, copper, and ammunition. Almost at once there was mutiny among the motley Turkish traders who had offered them escort on the twelve-days' journey.

Had it not been for the Bakers' faithful native boys, Richarn and twelve-year-old Saat—who overheard a plot to murder Baker and leave Florence to die in the jungles—they would have been killed. Only by keeping night and day armed vigil did they escape. It was with relief they watched the traitorous Turks finally abscond, muttering threats of vengeance if the Bakers followed them into the interior and spied on their cattle and slave stealing.

Fortunately, at a nearby native village, they happened on a chief, who in spite of his savage red ocher and grease make-up, proved to be both friendly and curious. Once it was clear to him that Samuel Baker was a white man who neither wanted to kidnap slaves nor steal cattle, he offered for hire seventeen of his own servants to replace the Turks. Then, without guide or interpreter, the Bakers set out again through jungles and deep ravines, into the interior.

Their progress was extremely slow. The natives, accustomed to lives of indolence, took little care of the overloaded caravan. Soon it developed, they had neglected to fill the water skins before starting. Then, too, the pet monkey Florence brought along amused itself by throwing away the black pancakes they had provided for their march.

The Bakers rode on ahead, anxious to find water. By the time they approached Illyria, their caravan was far in the rear. Tying their horses to a tree, Florence and Samuel sat down on a huge granite block, which had toppled from a mountain, to await their party. Like two honeymooners, they stared down on the valley. Mountains rimmed the village far below, while other villages, ringed by bamboo stockades, speckled the steep sides of the mountains. Suddenly they caught a glimpse of the Turkish caravan, with its sinister red flag with crescent, filing one by one through a narrow pass and entering Illyria. But to their relief, the Turks marched through the village, as if in a hurry, and disappeared.

As the Bakers resumed their journey on horseback, a body of natives suddenly appeared from the bushes, blocking the Bakers' path with raised bows and arrows.

"Who are you?" demanded their hunchback leader, in Arabic.

Samuel stared him down. "A traveler," he replied—also in Arabic.

"Do you want ivory?"

"No."

"You want slaves?"

"No, I do not want slaves."

"What countryman are you?"

"An Englishman."

The hunchback started at Baker's dark, bearded face. "You are a Turk!" he accused him.

"All right; I am anything you like."

The hunchback now turned his full attention to petite Florence, clad in boy's trousers and loose jacket, her blonde hair tucked up inside an oversize Eton cap.

"And that is your son?"

"No; she is my wife."

"Your wife? What a lie! He is a boy!"

"Not a bit. She is my wife who has come with me to see the women of this country."

"What a lie!"

He spat on the ground to show his disbelief, but let them pass peacefully.

Seven days later the Baker caravan reached Datouka, about one hundred miles from Gondokoro. Here they met the finest looking savages they had seen so far in Africa. Some were six feet tall, with fine physiques, pleasant faces, and good manners. Even though the Turkish caravan had preceded them here and raided their cattle, they allowed the Bakers to pass through their country safely.

They moved farther into the interior, crossed a mountain range and reached the Obbo country, 3600 feet above sea level. This was a land of dense grass jungle with wild grape vines and forests teeming with elephants. Here many of their animals died of tsetse fly bites. The natives, puny, badly fed, lazy, lived mostly on grain and wild yams which grew in many varieties in the Obbo jungle.

In this dreary land, both Florence and Samuel were taken ill with dysentery. While recovering in a squalid hut, a chief named Katchiba called on them, offering to take away their fever wih a magic spell. In this helpless condition, they soon found themselves pestered by rats, white ants, and snakes that he "charmed" into their hut.

Their last horse and camel now died, and only eight of their donkeys remained. There was an outbreak of smallpox among the natives, and soon many died of this disease. The wonder is that the Bakers recovered their own health.

Before resuming their journey, they were obliged to make

a final call on Katchiba. He received them in his "princely" residence, a large, circular hut, with door so low they had to crawl in. The king was the proud father of 116 children. He was a fine looking man, with straight military bearing. He sat on ox hides spread on the ground; Florence on his right, Samuel on his left. One of his numerous wives brought out native beer, and the Bakers sipped it out of a large gourd, the chief swallowing what remained. Then Katchiba played on a native harp, singing a wild, plaintive air. Next, he offered the Bakers the gift of a sheep. They politely refused it, but found it outside their hut when they returned.

Heartily sick of this country called Obbo, they wanted only to be on their way. But the ceremonies of leave-taking seemed endless. First, there were many exchanges of gifts; then visits from the wives of petty chiefs who could not get over Florence's long, blonde hair. They loved to watch her comb it. Nor could they get over her fair skin. However, they were critical of her appearance, suggesting she would improve her looks if she had her four front teeth extracted from the lower jaw, and did her hair up with a red ornament. They also suggested she pierce her under lip and insert a long pointed crystal about the size of a lead pencil in the hole.

"How many wives have you?" the chief's wife, Bokke, asked Baker. When he told her Florence was his only wife, she laughed in disbelief.

Finally, on January 5, 1864, Florence and Samuel Baker were permitted to go on their way. Florence was now riding an ox, a new experience for her. Almost as soon as they started, she was tossed over the head of the animal. The ox bolted, never to be seen again, taking with it an English saddle; Florence escaped with only minor bruises.

As the caravan continued its journey into the interior, the natives, especially the women, flocked from all parts of the dismal countryside to stare at Florence. They regarded her as a great freak. Many brought her presents of milk and flour, receiving beads and silk kerchiefs in exchange. Since a number of the porters had now deserted, the Bakers disposed of their tent, portable bath, rice, and coffee in order to lighten their caravan.

As they journeyed on, the Bakers made frequent inquiries from natives about the great body of water to the west of Unyoro. The chiefs they met shrugged their shoulders, pretending never to have heard of it, though it was obvious they had, or they evaded by saying that the water was much too far away. Besides, why, they asked, should white people make so long a journey to the country of the lakes merely to acquire knowledge. One asked, "Suppose you do get to the great water? What will you do with it? What will be the good of it? If you do find that the large river flows from it, what then?"

But on January 22, 1864—in spite of many false leads and setbacks—Florence and Samuel Baker had the thrill of reaching the first site to indicate they were on the right trail. They suddenly saw before them the sparkling White Nile. But even as they stared at it in awe, natives armed with spears watched them furtively from across the river.

They hurried on to Karuma, where the Nile flowed west between great rapids and high cliffs. Immense groves of bananas lined sharp ravines. There were beautiful palms bordering the river. Here the Nile was about 150 yards wide, gushing newborn from Victoria Lake. With great boldness, Baker dispatched one of his men across the lake in a canoe to spread the word: "Speke's brother has arrived with valuable presents for Kamrasi, your king."

The news soon spread like a forest blaze. Before long, the hostility of the natives turned to friendliness. They flocked around the Bakers, welcoming them by playing on lutes, singing and dancing for them.

But when Samuel Baker insisted on crossing the lake, he was told Kamrasi had given strict orders no stranger might cross his river.

It took an entire day to persuade the natives their expedition was a peaceful one. Then at length, with three attendants, Florence and Samuel were allowed to cross. The rest of the party crossed later. Once on the other side, Florence and Samuel were imprisoned in a squalid hut, the object of as much native curiosity as if they had been locked up in the zoo. And they were no closer to a meeting with the elusive Kamrasi than before.

As they waited day after day, the strain of the long hard journey, and the uncertainty as to its outcome, told on them. Then suddenly the "king" sent for them. At least Samuel Baker assumed he was being taken to the king when—too ill to walk now—he was carried by his men to the capital, and laid on a mat at the "king's" feet. He did not know until months later he was meeting not Kamrasi, but the king's brother. The real Kamrasi was in hiding, fearful that Baker was in league with the Turk traders. Florence accompanied her husband into the "king's" presence, fatigued and frightened.

The "king" was over six feet tall, dressed in a long robe of black cloth. He sat on a copper stone placed on a carpet of leopard skins. Through an interpreter, Baker made known the peaceful object of his journey. He began:

"The queen of my country takes a great interest in the discovery of the Nile source. Now it has proven to be within your dominion, and I wish to visit the lake and ascend to the junction and exit of the river that Speke, my brother, told me of."

"Ah—the lake is 'M'wootan,'" said the "king." Then, regretting having said this, he added: "But you might be murdered going there."

"No Englishman can be murdered without news soon reaching our queen. And if anything happened to me—"

"It is too far away," evaded the "king," "a six month's journey at least."

"That is not what my brother Speke told me."

"We shall think about it," said the "king."

Now began the usual exchange of gifts. Baker gave the chief a Persian carpet, red silk sash, pair of scarlet shoes, white cashmere mantle, large quantity of beads and a double-barreled gun. The gun took the "king's" instant fancy, and he began shooting it haphazardly, to the consternation of his subjects. Fortunately, he tired of this before anyone was wounded or killed. Then he gave Baker seventeen cows and quantities of fruit and cider. Next he showed him a present Speke had given him—a watch that wouldn't work.

"It is dead," said the "king," and sadly told of having poked it with a needle to explain its tickings to his subjects.

After begging more gifts from the Bakers—a Turkish sword, a belt, more beads, and even the kerchief with silver drops worn by Florence, he said coolly to Samuel Baker:

"I will send you to the lake; but you must leave behind your wife."

Ill though he was, Samuel Baker responded with great rage. Whipping out his pistol, he aimed it at the "king's" heart, and told "Kamrasi" in no uncertain terms that if he dared repeat this vile insult, he would kill him on the spot. Meanwhile Florence rose from her seat and, indignation wiping out her fears, made an excited speech in English. The "king" could not understand a single word, but her manner told him plainly she was no man's slave.

The "king" seemed astonished at the Bakers' outbursts. "Don't be angry," he pleaded. "I had no intention of offending you by asking for your wife. I will give you a wife if you want one, and I thought you might have no objection to give me yours. It is my custom to give my visitors wives, and I thought you might exchange. Don't make a fuss about it: I will never mention it again."

To placate the Bakers, he offered them an escort of about three hundred men to accompany them to the great lake. This escort was a bizarre one indeed—the men wore leopard and white monkey skins with cow tails attached. Some wore antelope horns on their heads, some false beards made of bunches of hair cut off cows' tails. They soon proved to be more nuisance than aid. Throughout the march, they sang, danced, screamed, capered, and staged sham battles. Nor did they pay the least attention to the caravan or the Bakers.

What with the blazing heat and the strange antics of their escort, it was little wonder that Florence Baker suddenly became desperately ill. She fell to the ground. Her teeth and hands were clenched; her eyes wide open. She stared blankly ahead. She was suffering a violent sunstroke, Samuel Baker knew, as he gently placed her on a litter and brought her to the nearest village. He placed her in a hut, keeping day and night vigil, nursing her constantly. Outside the wild escort grew ever more unruly.

Only by whipping out his pistol, and ordering them, in the most ferocious manner he could summon, to go home, did he finally get rid of them. He was relieved when they disappeared, and only a handful of his trusted porters remained with him.

Dispirited and ill himself, Samuel Baker now pushed on day after day, his wife lying insensible in the litter. At night, watching and nursing her in some hideous ant-plagued hut, with only the light of a lamp made of a broken water-jar filled with fat, and the howls of wild beasts lurking nearby, he had good reason to regret having permitted his beloved wife to come with him. There seemed no doubt now that Florence was dying.

As they continued the dismal journey, her condition seemed so hopeless that the porters looked about for a dry spot to dig her grave. Then, as they began digging and waited for what seemed her certain end, she made a slight change for the better. From wild, tossing delirium, she fell at last into a long restful sleep. Her breathing became normal.

When she awoke hours later, color had returned to her cheeks, and sparkle to her gray eyes.

"She is saved!" whispered Samuel Baker, kneeling beside her in gratitude. "God alone knows what helped her to recover!"

They rested for two days. When they resumed the march, Florence, again her own blithe self, was riding horseback.

Then, to add to their thankfulness, a native guide said to them one night, "We shall reach the great lake tomorrow!"

They could hardly sleep that night. At dawn, Florence and Samuel were in the saddle, eager to reach their goal.

That same day, March 14, 1864, the travelers stood on a high hill, the glory of their long sought prize before them. Far below lay a vast expanse of silvering water. This boundless sea glittered in the noonday sun. On the western horizon, distant mountains rose thousands of feet above the lake's level. This was the body of water never before viewed by white men, not even by John Speke and Captain Grant.

Their first impulse was to cheer. Instead, remembering the dangers and vagaries of their journey, he and Florence stood there silently, praising God for having guided them to their goal. They called the lake the Albert Nyanza, in memory of Queen Victoria's deceased husband, Prince Albert.

As he and Florence slowly descended the mountain slope to the water's edge, he braced himself with a bamboo stick. Florence clung to his shoulder. In two hours, they reached a pebbly beach. Then with sudden childish abandon, they both rushed into the lake. Tired and thirsty, their hearts grateful, they were the first white people to drink from the sources of the White Nile. It was a moment in their lives they never forgot.

Then they went on to Vacovia, a fishing village on the shore of the lake. There Baker bought an ox and two kids so that his men might have a feast to honor the discovery. When all was prepared, he addressed his thirteen dark-skinned companions.

"It is a great honor," he said, "for so small a number as we are to have achieved what we set out to do. I forgive you all your past offenses."

Up at sunrise, carrying a powerful telescope, he and Florence surveyed the lake, and made out two large waterfalls.

"The beach was perfectly clean sand on which the waves rolled like those of the sea, throwing up weeds precisely like seaweeds on an English shore," he wrote later. "It was a grand sight to look on this vast reservoir of the mighty Nile and to watch the heavy swell tumbling on the beach, while far to the southwest we searched as vainly for a bound as though upon the Atlantic. No European had ever trod upon the sand of that lake, nor had the eyes of a white man ever scanned its vast expanse of water. We were the first, and this was the key to the great secret even Julius Caesar yearned to unravel but in vain. Here was the great basin of the Nile, that received every drop of water, even from the passing shower to the roaring mountain torrent that drained from Central Africa towards the north. This was the great reservoir of the Nile."

It was true, he knew, that Speke and Grant were the first to trace the sources of the Nile to Victoria Nyanza, and make sure that the White Nile issued from the north end of that lake by way of Ripon Falls. But Florence and he now saw that this same stream proceeded northwest to Albert Nyanza. Now they must make certain it received a further

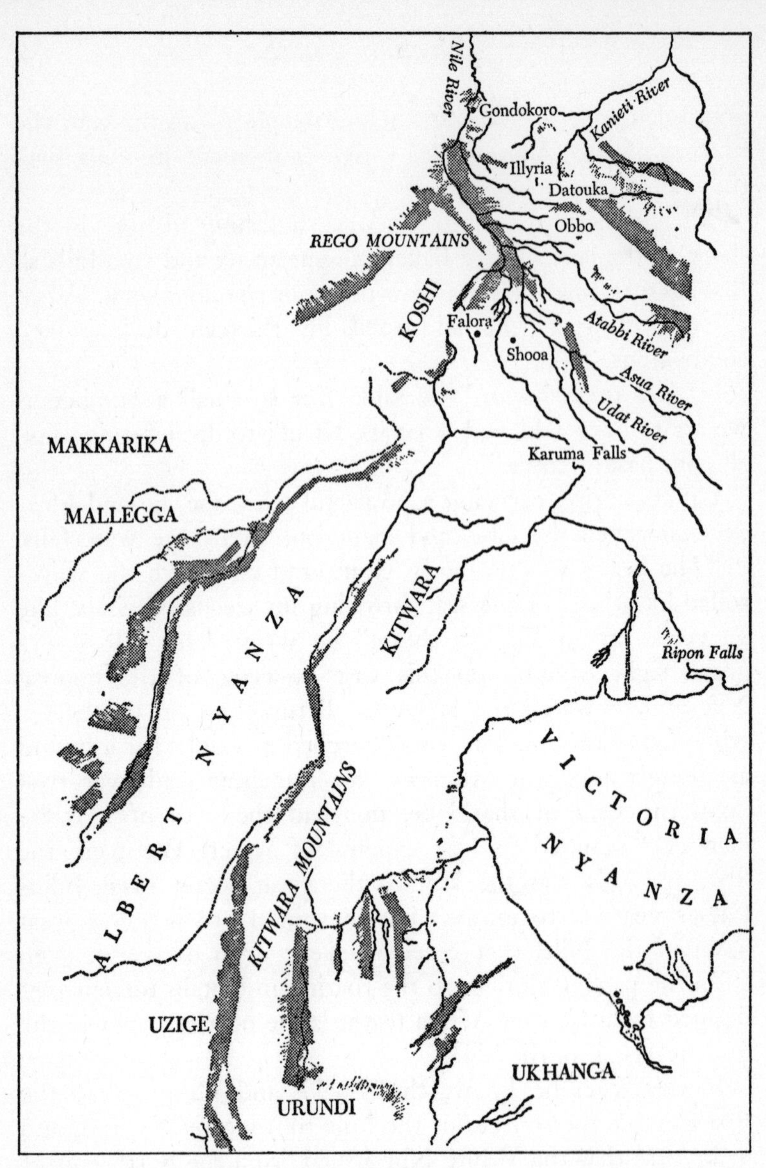

These are the regions through which the Bakers traveled on the way to Lake Albert (Albert Nyanza). This map is drawn from one which Baker prepared for the Royal Geographical Society. It is now considered rare.

supply of water from that lake, then continued north past Gondokoro on its way to Khartoum.

Eight days later, in native canoes, Florence and Samuel Baker explored the lake. Some parts of the shore were very steep, rising in high cliffs to a height of about 1500 feet. On the level embankments, swarms of crocodiles lay motionless in the sun, while waddling hippopotamuses waded into the water.

A gale came up. Swiftly it turned into a lashing storm. As thunder and lightning met, turning the lake into a resounding bowling alley, the Bakers rushed to the sandy beach. In spite of waterproof cabins, they were drenched to the skins.

Once back in their hut, they wrapped themselves in blankets before a roaring fire; then brought out rations, and enjoyed a good night's sleep on clean straw.

Next morning Baker killed a crocodile. His porters helped him cut it up for preservation, but refused to taste the rare tidbits. They would not eat reptile meat.

Although "King Kamrasi" had sent out a command to each village to supply rowers for the Baker expedition, the natives refused to go beyond the village next to theirs, fearing the slave traders. Now, for several days, no rowers volunteered to help the Bakers; when they finally found some and started out, they were obliged to change boatmen four times in less than a mile.

In spite of this snail-like pace, thirteen days later they reached the site where the White Nile issued from Albert Nyanza. Then they and their original escort of porters sailed down the river until blocked by a great cataract. It was the most spectacular waterfall of the Nile they had ever seen. The Bakers named it Murchison Falls after Sir Roderick Murchison, President of the Royal Geographical Society.

Samuel stayed at this site long enough to sketch the beautiful falls, while Florence made botanical records of the region. Then, leaving the canoes to drift down the river, the party began the slow overland return trip to Gondokoro by way of the banks of the Nile.

The return to Gondokoro was even more harrowing for Florence and Samuel Baker than their journey to Lake Albert had been. It was marked by tribal wars in the mixed-up domain of Kamrasi through which they were obliged to pass. It was marked, too, by near starvation and recurrent fevers which made them both despair of ever bringing their valuable findings to the attention of the Royal Geographical Society in England. Most of all, it was marked by ironic overtones.

At one time, Samuel Baker came to the aid of the cowardly Kamrasi, who, through his brother, asked Baker to protect him from both the Turkish raiders and hostile tribesmen. At Samuel Baker's command, the real Kamrasi came out of hiding to meet him in the king's courtyard. There Baker ordered the Union Jack to be hoisted and, dressed in a Highland costume, told the king that he and his country now had nothing to fear, for they were under full protection of England and could therefore stand off all invaders. His brave gesture worked, too! The Turkish raiders made peace with the king, and even brought peace offerings to the Bakers—letters and papers from Speke which had been sent to Gondokoro two years before. One was a paper, a copy of the *Illustrated London News*, with portraits of Speke and Grant, and a report of their Nile discoveries.

Then, as the happy king triumphed over his native enemies (and carried off the women and children into slavery himself!), the Bakers and their small party joined the Turkish caravan, a thousand in number, and reached Shoa safely, with the Union Jack leading the procession. There, native women danced in honor of the "brave white woman," Florence

Baker, and even the Turkish leader, Ibrahim, kissed her hand and said, "By Allah! No woman in the world has a heart so tough as to dare to face what you have gone through!"

They had set out for Gondokoro in February 1865. When, sometime later, they reached the outskirts, the Turkish traders parted with them reluctantly. Though the Bakers were more opposed to slavery than ever, the Turks trusted and respected them now. As the two explorers came into the squalid way station, the Union Jack mounted on a bamboo stick and carried in front of their little party, guns saluted them and natives shouted a welcome. Baker cried out, "Thank God! Hurrah! Three cheers for Old England and the Sources of the Nile." Florence threw her arms around her husband and hugged him.

Though they had left adequate money with an agent at Khartoum, there were no supplies and no boats waiting for the Bakers. They were forced to hire a decrepit vessel returning empty to Khartoum. Not until a plague broke out on board did the captain tell them there was a deadly plague at Khartoum, and many were dying of it. Although Florence and Samuel Baker were spared from contracting this dreadful disease, their beloved native boy, Saat, was stricken. Florence nursed him with tearful devotion, but he died. The boat stopped only long enough for him to be given a Christian burial on the sandy shores of the Nile.

It was during this return trip to Khartoum—remembering the terrible sights of slaves being taken from homes and families—that the Bakers swore to do all in their power, if they lived, to break up the awful traffic in human lives.

On May 5, 1865, the brave explorers reached Khartoum. It was a place of mourning. They were further saddened by news that their friend, John Speke, had died in England. Slowly they made their way to Suakin on the Red Sea, and from there were conveyed to Suez in an Egyptian transport.

For the first time in more than four years, they stayed at English hotels and had the delightful experience of sleeping in comfortable beds with clean linen sheets and soft pillows. Florence discovered that a new style in hairdress—the chignon—was now in vogue among fashionable European women. Starved for feminine frills, she took great pleasure in having her hair dressed in this latest fashion, though her husband confessed later he preferred her simple braided hairdo.

Before triumphantly returning to England, the Bakers found a situation for their faithful native servant, Richarn, in Cairo, and left money for his education in an English school being established there.

For having come to the relief of Speke and Grant, and completing their important discoveries, Samuel Baker was awarded a gold medal by the Royal Geographical Society. In 1866, a degree of M.A. was conferred on him by Cambridge University. Soon he was knighted, decorated by the khedive of Egypt, and awarded a gold medal by the Paris Geographical Society.

Florence Baker stood proudly with her husband, as honor after honor was conferred on him, happy in knowing she had been a vital part of his exploring life, as well as his beloved wife and companion.

Then, as Lady Baker, she returned with him to Egypt in 1867. With the Prince and Princess of Wales, they made a tour of the country the following year to take measures to abolish once and for all the insidious slave traffic.

In April, 1869, the khedive of Egypt bestowed the rank of pasha upon Samuel Baker, and presented him with a mandate, entrusting him with "the most supreme power, even that of death, and supreme authority over all those countries belonging to the Nile basin south of Gondokoro."

For the next four years, the brave exploits of the Bakers and their bodyguard of Egyptian soldiers, whom they called the "Forty Thieves," made them almost legendary figures throughout the civilized world.

Time after time, they broke up the sinister link between graft-ridden petty government officials of Egypt, Arabia, and Turkey and the native African chieftains, only to find new chains forged in this far-reaching, cancerous preying on human ignorance and misery. Even as some new local official was assuring Baker that the backbone of the slave trade had been destroyed, and Africa was now in good order, he and Florence would stand on the deck of their vessel, and see through a telescope tearful, pleading slaves being loaded on another ship. Every petty politician from Cairo to Fashoda, and far into the interior, was in league with the devil, it seemed.

On boarding a Nile vessel supposedly carrying an innocent cargo of ivory, Baker would find, hidden in the filthy hold, hundreds of wretched slaves—men, women, and children. Many of the children and women were linked by tight ropes passed from neck to neck, and suffering agony. In rage, Baker would order their fetters broken, put under arrest the officials responsible for the new outrage, and tell the weeping natives they were free to go home. But they shook their heads in mute terror, and told him they were afraid to return. Their villages had been burned to the ground, they sobbed. Most of their men had been slain; their cattle and corn stolen. When he assured them their villages would be rebuilt, and they would be given new supplies, they started back to their villages singing.

From one ravaged village to another, "Baker's men"—soldiers and sailors—went to rebuild the huts, plant vegetables and fruits, and keep the natives from inter-tribal warfare.

Then, at the Baker camp, the Union Jack would go up, and

a lantern-slide entertainment of Moses crossing the Red Sea would be put on for the instruction of the populace, as well as for the Mohammedan chieftains, who knew the story well.

Florence Baker became a shining symbol of womanly courage and virtue to the native women and children of many a nameless African village. While her husband wielded the "sword of righteousness" to bring to judgement the ringleaders of the traffic in slavery and end this human degradation, Florence worked on a more personal plane. She instructed the native women and children in domestic matters; taught them cleanliness and self-respect.

In August, 1873, Samuel Baker received the Imperial Order of the Osmanie, Second Class, in Cairo, for his services to Africa. Then he and Lady Baker returned to England, General Gordon succeeding him as pasha.

When her friends asked Lady Baker where they were going next, she sighed and said, "We have but one desire and that is to keep chickens in Devonshire." For a time, they did settle down in England at Sandford Orleigh, Newton Abbot, in Devonshire. While Lady Baker basked in a domestic life, her husband wrote of their adventures. But the wanderlust was still in their blood and, in 1879, they visited and explored Cyprus. From there they went to Syria, India, Japan, and America.

Until Samuel Baker's health began to fail in 1891, the Bakers and their daughter spent their winters away from England in Egypt and India. Then they settled down for good at Devonshire, and Lady Baker confessed she was glad.

There, in the comfortable great bedroom facing on their formal English garden, Lady Baker and their daughter nursed the ailing Samuel Baker. On December 30, 1893, he passed quietly away at the age of seventy-two.

Lady Baker stayed on for many years at Devonshire, living with personal memories more poignant and enduring to her than the medals, honors, and trophies they had won for their African explorations and achievements.

Sometimes she smiled, as she recalled the fierce Turkish leader, Ibrahim, who long ago had bowed to her, kissed her hand and said, "By Allah! No woman in the world has a heart so tough as to dare to face what you have gone through!"

As she walked in her English garden at evening, or "kept her chickens," she knew that her life of adventure with Samuel Baker had brought her few regrets and many deeply satisfying experiences.

DELIA J. DENNING AKELEY

The outstanding news story of the exploring world in 1924 was that the Brooklyn Museum was sending a "one white woman" expedition to Central Africa. With only a Somali interpreter and gunbearer, and a few natives picked up during the course of her explorations, this woman would travel up the Tana River, cross the Somali Desert, and penetrate the Budongo Forest and Jubaland. She would live among little-known tribes in the East and, following the course of the crocodile-infested Congo River, come out in a year or more—if lucky—by way of western Congo.

Could a woman on her own endure the dangers and loneliness of jungle living? Could she gain better insight than a man explorer into the daily lives of native women and children? Could she actually find the elusive forest Pigmies of the wild Ituri forest? These were some of the questions the museum wanted answered. She must also collect valuable specimens of the rapidly disappearing wild mammals of Africa en route.

The woman entrusted with this dangerous assignment by Dr. George P. Engelhardt, curator of the museum, was not a young woman. She was a soft-spoken, charming woman in her middle or late fifties, a cultivated woman with white hair, gray eyes behind pince-nez glasses, delicate features, and a wry sense of humor. She was, however, no novice in African explorations.

Her name was Delia Akeley. For more than twenty years, she had been the wife and helpmeet at home and on safaris of Carl Ethan Akeley, African explorer, taxidermist, naturalist, inventor, and sculptor. She had accompanied him on two important expeditions to Africa, one in 1905 and again in 1909.

Carl Akeley was well known as the "wonder boy" of the museum world. Born on a farm at Clarendon, New York, in 1864, he started work as a youth of nineteen with the Ward Museum in Rochester. He went on from there to the Museum of Milwaukee and then to the newly opened Field Museum of Chicago. It was while in Chicago that he met and married Delia Denning on December 23, 1902. In 1909, he and Delia came to New York, where he worked out from the Museum of Natural History.

His experiments with small habitat exhibits, showing muskrats, deer, and especially the wild African elephant in natural surroundings of jungle grass, exotic flowers and foliage, soon transformed taxidermy from a crude trade to an art.

In connection with his work as taxidermist, Akeley also became a fine sculptor of wild life. One of his bronze pieces,

"The Old Lion," was so well liked by the Akeleys' long-time friend, Theodore Roosevelt, that after he left the White House, the former president kept it on his desk in his Oyster Bay, Long Island, home to remind him of an African safari he had gone on with the Akeleys in 1909. Akeley's sculptured piece on a gorilla, "The Chrysalis," was the subject of endless controversy in religious circles and in the press of the twenties. The controversy reached a climax when the Reverend Potter displayed the work of art in his modern church in New York to demonstrate lectures on the evolution of man from the ape. This attracted capacity crowds. Akeley was also known for his inventions of the Akeley Cement Gun, used for mounting wild life, and the Akeley Camera, considered by naturalists the best motion picture camera ever devised. To the general public, he was most famous as an African explorer, beginning with his first expedition to Somaliland in 1896, when Africa was still an unknown continent to most Americans.

Until Carl and Delia Akeley were divorced in March, 1923, she had completely submerged herself in the dedicated life of her brilliant husband.

"Mickey," as she was called by her intimates, was known and beloved in museum circles as a gracious hostess to celebrities and non-celebrities alike. In the Akeleys' well-run, but modest apartment not far from the New York Museum of Natural History, she presided over fund-raising social affairs for many years. Here, too, friends from out of town dropped in—Orville Wright, George Eastman, Theodore Roosevelt, and many others. Often, the pet monkey of the childless Akeleys, "J.T.," entertained them. J.T. was named after John T. McClutcheon, famous cartoonist of the Chicago *Tribune*, who had been with Ake and Mickey in Africa when they came across the lovable monkey.

Mickey rarely talked about herself and her girlhood as

Delia Denning in Beaver Dam, Wisconsin, but she had a knack of drawing other people out, even her somewhat taciturn and ailing husband, who lived but for his work.

When she was still a young woman, Mickey's hair became prematurely white. Only a few knew that it turned white during her second expedition to Kenya, Africa, with her husband in 1909. She nursed him through malaria, blackwater fever, and just barely brought him through alive when he was badly mauled and his face disfigured for life by a wounded, enraged elephant.

Only a few knew that Mickey single-handedly shot down the biggest lion ever to be brought back from Africa and mounted in the New York Museum of Natural History.

Only a few knew that she, more than any other person, encouraged Carl Akeley to go on with his dream of creating the lifelike Akeley African Hall, which has brought a primeval Africa of free roving wild life no longer in existence to countless school children and adults who now troop through the New York museum. To further this dream, they endured many personal privations, even selling the home they planned for retirement—their farm in upstate New York—to help complete their 1909-11 expedition.

And only a very few knew of the great courage it took for Delia Akeley to begin life again without Ake, knowing that soon he would remarry.

Twinkling gray eyes, filled with interest in the future, met reporters who saw her off when she left New York on August 23, 1924. It was a "poor man's expedition," she told them, just before setting sail for England, en route to Mombasa, Africa. If there were any millionaires around, she hoped they would remember the hard-pressed museums in their wills. When asked about remembering explorers, she replied, "They are used to personal sacrifice. They thrive on it."

»»

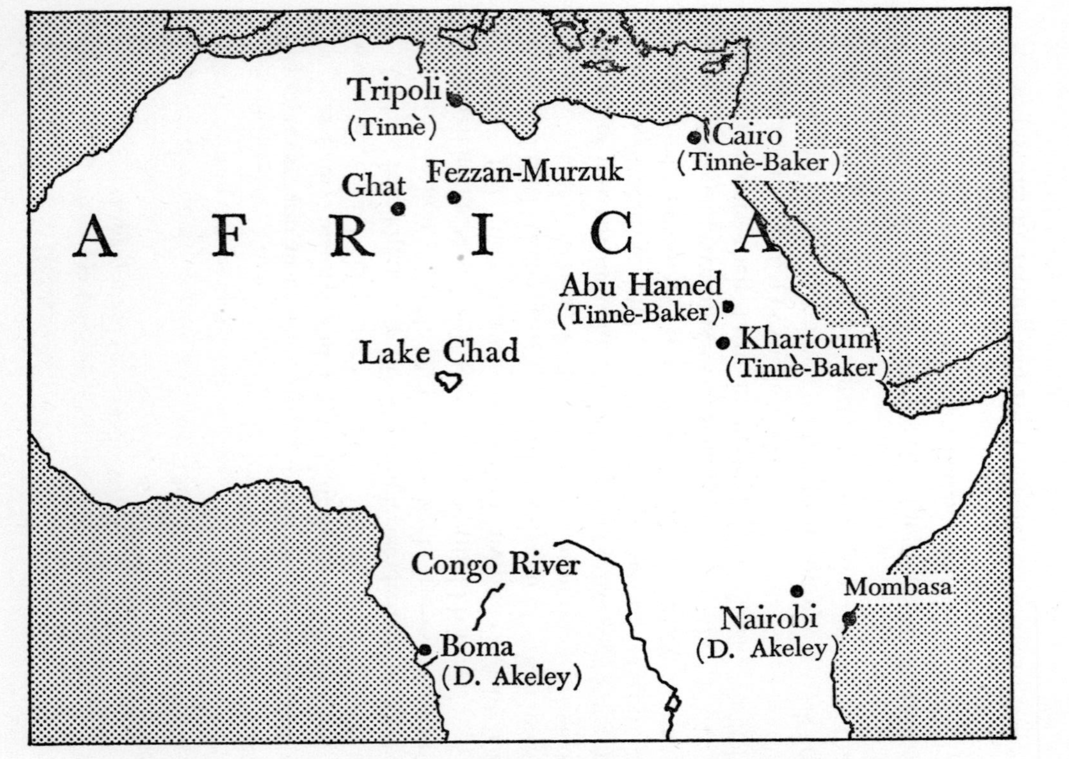

North and Central Africa, showing some of the places visited by Alexine Tinnè, the Bakers and Delia Akeley.

In spite of her experience as an explorer, there was skepticism in some quarters at the museum's sending a woman alone, and especially this gentle-appearing lady no longer young, on so dangerous a journey. Both Dr. Engelhardt and the public anxiously awaited news of Delia Akeley in the weeks that followed.

It was with a sigh of relief that George Engelhardt received his first cable from Delia in December saying all was well. She had arrived in Mombasa late in October and traveled inland to establish headquarters at Nairobi, Kenya. It had changed since she went there with her husband in 1905, and first saw it as a hamlet of tin houses, many black people, Hindus, and a scattering of white men.

Her equipment included the usual outfit of big game hunters—supplies, weapons, and cameras for still and motion pictures. But her expedition differed essentially from the others in that her only companions on the trip into the interior would be natives selected and trained by her alone. However, because of her past experiences, she assured him, she was as convinced as ever that the natives, if treated with tact and kindness, would respond by giving loyalty and dependable aid. She still believed, because of her previous studies of primitive tribes, that it was actually easier for a woman than for a man explorer to gain their trust.

After this cablegram, the museum waited impatiently for further word, late in March, 1925, *The New York Times* sounded an alarm:

"Mrs. Delia Akeley, on an expedition to study child life in the jungles, has not been heard from in three months," said the newspaper. "Anxiety is felt for her by officials of the Brooklyn Museum of Arts and Science.

"Since a cablegram received by the museum early in December, she has not been heard from directly. Weeks ago a news agency reported Mrs. Akeley was ill with ptomaine poisoning, according to George P. Engelhardt, the museum's curator. He believes the explorer became ill while making her first advance toward the section in which she expected to begin her work and was taken back to Nairobi in Kenya district, about two hundred miles from Mombasa. It was at Nairobi Mrs. Akeley had intended to establish her headquarters of a native caravan."

The anxiety felt by museum and public alike continued into late April. Then, a letter reached George Engelhardt with an African postmark. He opened it, delighted to see Delia Akeley's familiar handwriting again. It was dated March 12, and written from Kisumu, Kenya Colony, East Africa. He read:

"Dear Mr. Engelhardt:

Many thanks for your encouraging letter of September last and the ones enclosed. I received them about six weeks ago upon my arrival at Nairobi. Upon receipt of the letters I went off at once on another safari after the hyena and a reedbuck which I failed to get down the Tana.

"I also neglected writing until I could tell you that I had shipped through Safari Ltd. most of the specimens asked for by the Museum. Unfortunately, I lost several fine skins on the Tana, owing to constant ducking by the rain and my careless canoemen. Among these were a Peter's-eye gazelle, an antbear, a porcupine and my prize specimen, my one and only kudu (a large handsome antelope) which went overboard with the men when a giant lizard dropped from the limb of a tree and took possession of the boat.

"I only saw two kudu on the whole trip, so you can appreciate my feelings. To hunt for them in other parts meant asking for special privilege and taking out a sportsman's license which would cost $500. The special license which the Government had very graciously given me with permission to enter the closed Tana district had expired. The Governor, Sir Robert Crayndon, who was my friend, died before I reached Nairobi, and I hadn't the courage to ask favors of the acting Governor whom I did not know personally. This is just a bit of hard luck which I hope to compensate with something better in the Congo.

"However, I am sending with the collection what I believe will be of far more interest and of great value to the Museum —bottled specimens of the hairless mole. I believe these specimens will be the first to reach America, in fact, there are only a few specimens in Europe. I worked with my boys day after day without success until finally I offered a reward of 10 shillings for them. Then a little Somali boy sat over a hole the better part of a day before he finally speared two. Apparently they never come above the surface of the ground. They dig their runways in places two and three feet below the surface and their runways branch out from the main passage in all directions like tributaries of a river. These strange little animals are perfectly at home in the water. One of those brought in was alive. I put it in a pail of water where it swam about or rested on the bottom for over two hours without any sign of drowning. I could not keep it there longer for I was getting ready to move camp. I found their kind active for about a mile west of the Kinna River and there they stopped abruptly and the common mole of East Africa took their place. I am sending the measurements of the specimens and I am also sending a few curios and a bundle of poisoned spearheads and arrows, mostly gifts from natives.

"I am traveling as light as possible across the Congo on account of difficulties in getting porters. I have paid Safari Ltd. for packing and shipping trophies to Mombasa and from there the collection will go C.O.D. as you suggested or agreed. Everything is very expensive here and without my former experiences I would never be able to carry on. The country is being settled so fast that in a few years, a *very* few years, it will be too late.

"My journey up the Tana and across the Somali desert was

wonderful. It is practically the only part of British East Africa left untouched and the reason is that it is a difficult country to reach, unhealthy, and the desert country is inhabited by hostile natives and is still under military rule. The Officials were going to call me back because the Somalis had murdered a white official a few days before I started. But I got off before word came.

"I was very ill on the Tana and thought for a few days that I was paying Africa's price for my boldness. Tinned food was the cause, however, and I recovered in due time, although I lost 40 pounds in weight. I hired camels from the Somalis in San Kuri and had my very own camel caravan crossing the desert. I traveled under the stars with no tent over me and felt like a Bedouin and loved it. No experience I have ever had equals it.

"Just at the present time the Government is sending troops to punish the Somalis who are fighting just east or northeast of the country I passed through. The same people are the ones who came across the border and raided and killed the natives. The Army men said they would never dream of going out without 35 or 40 Askaris (soldiers) with them. Well, frankly, the knowledge added spice to my journey.

"I plan to go north to Kilo and from there to Pigmy country, then northwest into the French Congo, then northeast to Nigeria and Lake Chad. From there I shall either cut across to the railway or come out by way of the Niger River. I shall in that long journey come across some very interesting tribes.

"I want to be remembered to Dr. Fox and all good friends at the Museum and with kind regards to both Mrs. Engelhardt and you, I am,

Yours very sincerely,
Delia J. Akeley"

Several months later, Delia Akeley sat in a leaky Congo "rest hut" waiting for the incessant rains to let up. She wondered if George Engelhardt had ever received the letter she dispatched to Nairobi via a native porter, in March. The porters she engaged meant well, but only one or two compared with her trusted tent-boy Ali and other faithful servants who had been with her on previous African expeditions. However, they were the best she could get.

Now that she was in the jungles, she would be cut off from all contact with civilization until her return to the coast in late summer or fall. If she returned. One never knew.

Since she entered the Congo at Boma, bound for the Ituri forest, there had been no time to worry. Now, there was little to do but stare at the mud walls, with the remarkable native drawings of birds, beasts, and reptiles, as millions of mosquitoes stormed the close-mesh mosquito netting tacked over the hole of a window. What with mosquitoes, tiny black flies, and fleas on the rotting grass roof and in filth left on the earthen floor by former occupants of the hut, what with rats, spiders, thousand-legged worms, toads, and centipedes, the underlying fear, which was always with one in Africa, was back again in full measure. It had been there in 1905 and again in 1909. In depressed moments, she had begged Carl Akeley to take her home and let her keep house for the rest of her life.

She took up notebook and pencil and began to write with grim determination, by light of a kerosene lantern. Now and then she scratched out a word, or replaced an entire line. She had the hollow feeling that she might be writing words in the sand. How many explorers and missionaries before her had been devoured by this Dark Continent without a trace!

"Of all the many agencies that combine to try the courage of a lone woman traveling in Africa," wrote Delia Akeley, "there is nothing to my mind more trying than to be in one of these old Congo rest houses in the rainy season when it is cold and disagreeable, with one's morale low, and when one is wondering what sort of complex prompted one's straying so

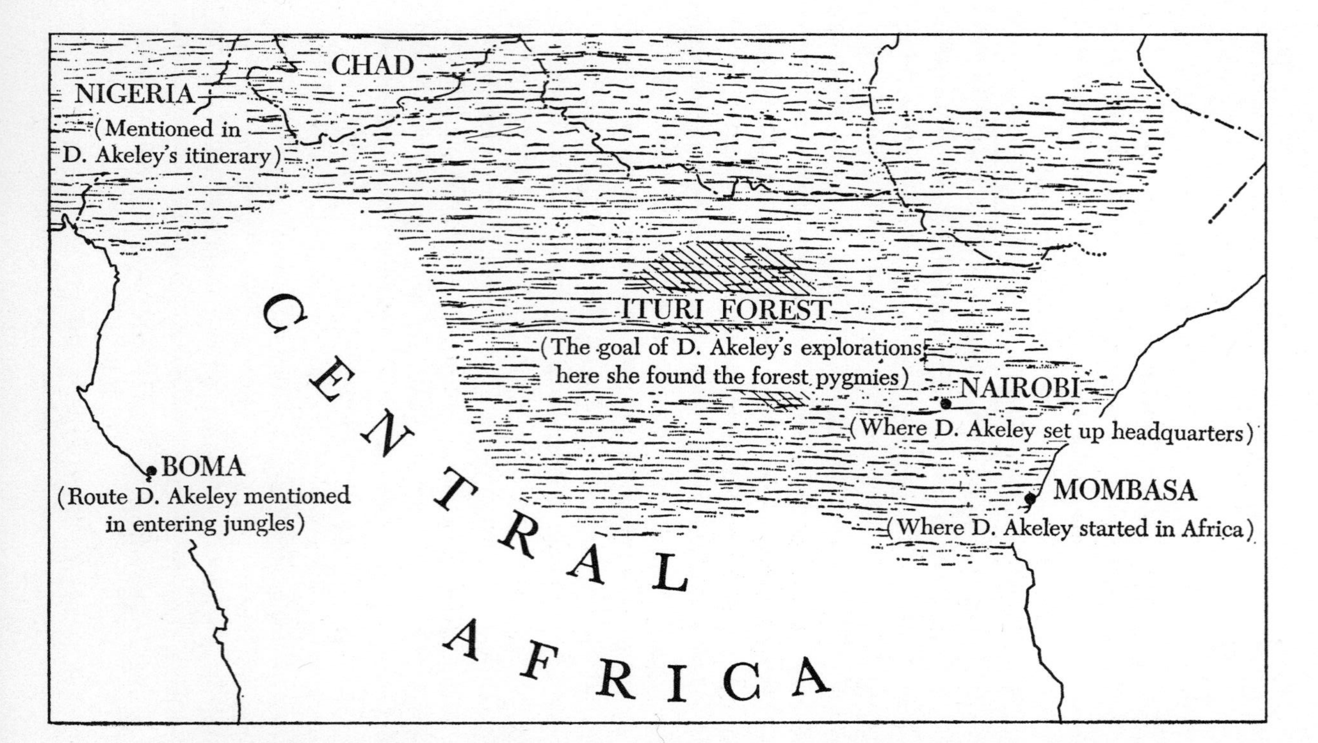

Central Africa and the Ituri Forest. It was here that Delia Akeley found the little known tribe of forest Pigmies.

far from the comfort and luxuries of civilization. Indeed, it takes courage to go to sleep in one of these firetraps, with bats, insects and snakes for companions—with lightning flashing, as the thunder booms and crashes and rocks the insecure mud walls, while termites and white ants gnaw on the poles of your hut.

"The first Pigmies I met since entering the Congo were brought in from their forest home by a friendly Sultan in whose village I stayed. As soon as they saw me take out my camera, my guests lined up and began to pose, proving beyond doubt they were in the habit of posing for all travelers who passed their way. They were not the Pigmies I had come so far to see!"

Delia glanced up from her notebook, and listened for a few moments to the howl of a hyena. She closed her eyes to shut out the gloom of her present abode. Since the morning when she and her little band of porters had begun the long weary march—going deeper and deeper into the heart of the boundless forest in search of the unknown Pigmies—a weird sense of being swallowed up by another age and clime had been with her.

At first, in good weather, they camped at night in the clearings where the friendly Walesse had their villages and where she could buy food for herself and her porters. But then the woodland trail, packed hard by passing generations of bare feet, wound through the great moss and liana-draped forest, over wooded hills, across networks of rivers and through gruesome swamps where her carriers struggled and floundered and sank waist deep in the oozy black mud.

She was about ready to give up when one day, while passing through a village, she came on a group of tiny women dancing. The Walesse village sultan sat beneath the *barasa* (veranda) of a hut watching the dancers. The women were stupidly drunk and the perspiration rolled off their bodies. She watched them as they went round and round in a circle, yelling and shouting, and keeping time by pounding the earth with their bare feet. They had imbibed so much palm wine that they seemed unaware of her presence until she focused her camera on them. Unlike other tribes, these little people stared at the camera, without comprehending what it was. Then, with wild terrified shouts, they ran behind the hut and, leaping over logs and ant heaps, disappeared into the forest like frightened antelopes.

Finally, some were coaxed back, and she won their friendship by giving them salt and letting them look at themselves for the first time in a mirror. She knew that these were the forest Pigmies she had been searching for so long. They had come out of hiding, furtively visiting the Walesse village to exchange elephant meat and skins for vegetables, bananas, and palm wine. But when she made inquiry as to where their own village was, the natives shrugged. Then they told her it was much too far away.

Determined to locate their hideout, she instructed one of her "boys," a small lithe runner, to follow them when they left, and trace them to their forest village, if he could.

"Tell their Sultan I will bring him gifts of tobacco and salt, if he will permit me to visit him. Let him know I am not a government official," she urged. For well she knew that all the natives were wary of these outsiders who wanted to change their lives.

The runner had gone and returned. He claimed to have found their village. But he was vague about what transpired. Their language was strange, he said evasively. Besides, he was too frightened of their poisoned arrows to approach their hideout.

Now she sat in this forsaken Congo hut, waiting for the rain to stop so that she could follow her little guide back into the Ituri forest. She only hoped he really did know where the Pigmies' hideout was.

She sighed, and returned to her notebook. "There is something indescribably weird and frightening about the Congo forest," she wrote, "for while it holds and fascinates, it also terrifies. After I had been in the forest a few weeks, there were times when a horrible feeling of oppression took possession of me and the forest seemed like prison walls. This feeling came upon me after a hard day's march through a tropical downpour or when I came into a village just after someone had died and the women were wailing their dismal death dirge. I felt as if I must push aside the walls of green which loomed so dark on every side and get out to the sunshine and wind-swept veldt again.

"It is difficult to describe the mixed fear and determination as I wait here now to follow my little guide into the Ituri forest again. For I must set out tomorrow to find the forest Pigmies, rain or no rain . . ."

Almost as soon as Delia started her journey next morning, her loose-fitting khaki trousers and jacket were soaked to the skin. Her clothing clung to her body, revealing how thin she had grown since her bout with ptomaine poisoning on the Tana River.

Mile after mile she followed her guide through the dripping, rainsoaked forest, while her other porters followed reluctantly. So dense was the trail that although it was day, she could see scarcely a yard in front of her. Often her glasses became blurred. She took them off and wiped them from time to time, but they were more bother than use to her at times such as this.

They crossed many small streams and swamps, and detoured around fallen giant trees which had been rotting there for ages. Moss, ferns, and strikingly beautiful orchids blanketed their gray, ghoulish trunks. But now, thank heavens, the rain was letting up at last. Still shivering, Delia went on with lighter heart. Sometimes it was hard to keep up with the gnomelike little native who slid through the forest ahead of her like a shadow, but keep up with him she did.

Twisted ropes of lianas sometimes caught her round neck and arms and enmeshed her rifle. As she untangled herself and rifle, she stumbled on. She could almost sense the spirits of past explorers lost in these jungles many years ago. One of them, Sir Henry Stanley, lived through the experience, and recorded the feeling of the jungle. His descriptions were true, she knew, as she experienced the same awe he felt at the luxuriant foliage combining with that of trees sixty meters in height obscuring all sunlight; as she saw the great herds of elephants trumpeting and squealing and smashing their way about, the buffalo and pig and forest antelope and monkeys, from smallest bush-baby monkey to great gorilla whose roar equaled that of the lion.

Suddenly she came to a clearing. This, then, was the home of the elusive forest Pigmies, that home probably never before visited by white man or woman. She, Delia Akeley, had found her way to their hidden village at last!

Her arrival caused little stir to anyone but herself. The sultan, a dwarf with heavily-bearded face and hairy chest, continued to sit impassively on an ebony stool before a fire. He drank palm wine from a big black pot. Unlike sultans of other tribes she had visited, he made no move to rise or come to meet her. Behind him some of the villagers, about twenty-one men, women, and children, stood. Their large eyes pierced her. They had bullet-shaped heads and broad flat noses. They ranged in color from yellowish brown to black. As she approached, a child peeked out at her shyly from between the legs of an elder. With rapidly beating heart, she stood under a great tree and gazed at the group. The men were armed with elephant spears. The boys carried small fur-covered bows and heavily barbed, steel-tipped arrows. Her first inclination was to turn and run. But recovering some of her will, she forced herself to walk slowly forward to the fire.

The sultan still did not rise. However, he reached out his dirty, hairy, but well-shaped hand, and began to jabber away in a language neither she nor her native boys could understand. At the same time, he pointed to another ebony stool which he had placed beside his own. No sooner did she sit down than he filled a gourd with wine. He took a sip to let her know it was not poisoned, then passed it to her. She pretended to drink. Next, she handed the cup to her tent-boy. The boy drained it, smacking his lips.

While her boys put up her tent and unpacked, the Pigmies watched curiously, and she had a chance to look over the village. The huts were of the usual beehive shape she had seen before, built in a circle around a cleared space. They were crudely made by drawing young saplings together, then covering them with leaves and binding the whole with young vines. It was obvious they were used only to sleep in or to sit in when it rained for they had no furniture. Indeed, she could find no furniture elsewhere, other than the ebony stools.

From the day Delia Akeley came upon the "little people" of the Ituri forest until the day she left them more than three months later, she entered into their daily life. She sat with them in the cleared space—their commons. She danced with them occasionally, and even attended their palavers (conferences). Although she had no interpreter who understood their language, she soon was able to make herself clear to them through sign language. And the longer she stayed, the more she understood their strange formless tongue.

Though they proved to be loveable people, she had to admit they seemed lacking in originality and intelligence. Their cooking utensils were of the crudest sort and they had no furniture to speak of. Even their spears and bows and arrows were obtained from blacksmiths of other tribes. They slept on skins of wild animals, and roasted their food on sticks over a fire.

They were perfectly at home in the forest, and she was reminded of stories she had read in childhood of sprites and elves. However, when she got to know them better, she deplored their lack of cleanliness, and made what seemed to her rather futile attempts to help them improve their sanitary standards. They seemed to hate bathing, even though they were fascinated by the improvised shower baths Delia took.

Their potbellied children ran around the forest practically naked, but neither cold nor rain bothered them. She saw no evidences of coughs or colds. They seemed to be strong, healthy, and well proportioned. Though children and adults alike were unwashed and odorous, they seemed free of those dreadful diseases so common to other Congo tribes.

On special occasions, the adults wore leaves or bark cloth fastened about the waist by a belt of grass cord. They wore no ornaments, and never mutilated their bodies or filed their teeth, as did some tribes. Living far away in the forest, apart from the influence of more "modern" Pigmies, they lived mostly by hunting. However, when they wanted weapons, tobacco, or palm wine, they stealthily secured them from other tribes, giving them in exchange ivory, skins of wild animals, and meat. Because of these visits to other tribes, a few of the Pigmies were over five feet, the obvious offspring of intermarriage with larger natives.

Once the women overcame their shyness, they showed greater curiosity about Delia Akeley than did the men. So much so that throughout her stay with them, one of her boys had to be constantly on guard to protect her belongings.

But though the men tipped their spears and arrows with vegetable poison brewed from leaves of a special vine, Delia was never the object of their deadly weapons. Indeed, though she had heard many rumors that these people were fierce—even cannibals—she saw no proof of this.

Only once was there an indication of this sort. That was when a child of six, swinging from the limb of a great tree, was given a playful push by a man Pigmy. The child swung through space wildly, then crashed against a tree trunk and was instantly killed. The mother of the child took his tiny crushed body to her hut, wailing in grief and outrage. Throughout the night Delia heard sounds of her sorrow. But next morning, the body was gone, and the incident seemed forgotten. Delia's tent-boy insisted the Pigmies had eaten the child, as was their custom.

One thing became clear. They were not selective in their eating habits, for their diet included snails, slugs, and long hairy caterpillars. They did not, however, impose their taste on Delia Akeley, and when she roasted meat or corn over her campfire, they never begged for her rations. But sometimes she shared them with these always hungry little people.

As first, the men went on hunting expeditions alone. But when they discovered that Delia was a better marksman than they, she was soon invited to go along with them. Twice while hunting with them, they ran off and left her to face stampeding herds of buffaloes. As agile as monkeys, they climbed great ropelike vines suspended from trees, while she held the herds at bay with her rifle until they turned and fled.

After these incidents, Delia was regarded more highly by the Pigmies than their witch doctors. For like all primitive tribes in Africa, the Pigmies were highly superstitious, and believed firmly in witchcraft. Just before an elephant hunt, or before a child was born, their medicine men held elaborate ceremonies, sprinkling the blood of birds and animals over charms. These were then worn by the hunters or mothers-to-be.

Only once was Delia Akeley's life in danger from the Pigmies. That was when she interfered in a family quarrel. The Pigmies practiced polygamy, just as did other African tribes, and the men thought nothing of beating their wives with or without cause. Usually a quarrel began because of jealousy among the wives, but on this occasion it began when the sultan's favorite wife dropped a choice bit of fat into the fire and could not retrieve it. Howling with rage, he knocked his wife down, striking her hard in the face. As he seemed on the point of killing her, Delia picked up the tiny man. Kicking and squirming, she set him down some yards away from his wife. Then he stamped his feet, and let out a torrent of angry words. Delia thought it time to say her prayers, but before poisoned darts were hurled her way, his wife restored peace and calm by offering the sultan another piece of fat she had taken from one of her children.

On the whole, her relations with the Pigmies were very friendly. The women especially confided in Delia, and on occasions let her act as midwife during childbirths. They were astonished to find how much her nursing improved their comfort at such times. At night, when she sat beside her own campfire, they often came over from their own, squatting on their heels on logs of wood, talking, drinking, and laughing, while the menfolk smoked the native tobacco she offered them.

Her last night with them was a touching experience. They knew she would leave them soon, for her boys were busy breaking up her camp and packing. They tried in their little-people way to keep her with them, imitating the noises of wild beasts in order to show her the great dangers she faced in the forest without them to protect her with their poisoned arrows. When she remained unconvinced, they tried hiding some of her belongings.

As she bid them a final good-by next morning, there were tears in the eyes of even the men Pigmies. Then, to her astonishment and delight, one of the tiny women asked in hesitant English, "When will you return, white Mem-sahib Clean-it-up?" She had thought the Pigmies incapable of learning; now she knew better.

»»

Delia Akeley returned to America alive and in good spirits late in October, 1925. As reporters met her on board the Cunard liner, the *Francania*, and later sat with her before a big map in the office of Dr. Engelhardt at the Brooklyn Museum, she told them some of her adventures. Out of her personal experiences and observations in African exploration, she brought a message to America.

Officials in Africa, she said, were sometimes immature in their dealings with the natives. In their efforts to turn them to "honest work," they often did more harm than good. She hoped they would leave the forest Pigmies alone for awhile —for they were the last sprites and elves left on earth!

Later, Delia showed the reporters her collections of big mammals, including many fine specimens of antelopes, gazelles, lions, hyenas, waterbucks, duikers, and dik-diks. All of these had reached the museum in excellent condition, then went through the process of tanning, and were ready for mounting.

The reporters went away, more amazed than ever by this beautifully groomed lady with gentle manners, who had crossed the African wilds with only native porters, then returned triumphant.

Headlines such as this appeared in New York papers:

"Lone Woman Feted in Jungle Sewing Circles." The story went on to say: "Wherever the white mem-sahib, better known as Mrs. Delia J. Akeley appeared, she met only old-fashioned hospitality. Wives of prominent Pigmies paid calls, dances were given for her in liana-draped ballrooms and she was received by the 'Sultana's' maidens arrayed in their most elegant vegetable finery.

"No woman before Mrs. Akeley has traveled alone, and so informally, through the heart of the dark continent from Lama to Matsdi. None has been received with more intimate cordiality by its exclusive 'sets.' "

And none understood their true needs better than she did.

»»

Delia Akeley went to Africa once more in 1929, remaining there a year. She visited the little forest people again, bringing companions this time. But her main purpose in returning to Africa was to visit the grave of her former husband, Carl Akeley.

He had died at Kabale, Uganda, November 16, 1926, while establishing a gorilla sanctuary near Mount Mikino for the Belgian government. According to his wishes, he had been buried in the heart of the Dark Continent.

It must have been a sad journey in some ways for Delia because another woman, his second wife, Mary Jobe Akeley, had accompanied Carl on his last African expedition. Whatever her thoughts as she stood on the ice-capped slopes of those beautiful mountains where she and Carl once stood, planning African Hall with youth and enthusiasm, she was her usual cheerful self on her return to America.

Soon after, she slipped out of the limelight. When she died some years later, few people—even in museum circles—recalled Delia Akeley's important role as an American explorer: first, as the long-time wife and companion of Carl Akeley, then as a woman past her youth who set out all alone to conquer an African jungle and her own loneliness. And in so doing, Delia Akeley discovered the hearts of the little people of the Ituri forest.

FANNY BULLOCK WORKMAN

Climb the highest mountain! Fanny Bullock Workman did just that when in 1906, at the age of forty-seven, she set a new record in mountain climbing. In skirts, and without oxygen equipment, she made the first ascent of a Nun Kun peak in the Kashmir region of the Himalayas, reaching an altitude of 23,300 feet. The record she set remained for many years unchallenged. Not until the 1930's was it broken, and not until 1953 was Mount Everest—5,729 feet higher than Nun Kun—successfully scaled for the first time by a New Zealand explorer and a Sherpa guide. This highest peak in the Himalayas, between Tibet and Nepal, was also the highest peak in the world.

In 1889, thirty-year-old Fanny set off with her ailing husband, William Hunter Workman, on a leisurely round-the-world bicycle trip, with no idea she would make any mountain-climbing records either in the Alps or in the wild Himalayas. But by the time they had introduced bicycles for two to Spain, climbed the mountains of Sicily, the Tyrol, Switzerland, and visited Japan, Ceylon, Java, Sumatra, Indochina, Burma, and India, Fanny and William were veteran travelers. They were also veteran mountain climbers.

A decade later, they spent two summers among the higher Himalayas to escape the heat of the Indian plains. They made an expedition from Srinagar, the capital of Kashmir, cycling into the mountains of Ladakh, Nubra, and Suru, and liked it so well that in the autumn they cycled from Darjeeling into Sikkim. In July, 1899, starting again from Srinagar, they crossed Deosai Plains into Baltistan. From Skardu they went to Shigar Valley over the Skoro La to Askole. On the occasions when the Workmans made trips by bicycle, they rode along paths where only ponies, oxen and the buffalo-like yaks had gone before. They were a source of amazement to the scattered populace. Few natives had ever seen bicycles before, and the bicycles of this era, with their monster-like front wheels, were bizarre indeed!

By the turn of the century, they had formed a permanent friendship with the exciting country of the Himalayas.

In eleven expeditions to the Himalayas, the first in 1899, Fanny and her husband became internationally famous as explorers of this little-known and, until they arrived, little-mapped region of the world. Together they explored and mapped the Biafo, the Chogo Lungma, the Hispar, the Baltoro, and the Soachen Glaciers, and climbed Koser Gunge, Mount Chogo, and Lungma.

Although William accompanied Fanny on the formidable Nun Kun climb, too, Fanny went on ahead with her Italian guide and one porter on the last lap of the journey to the top. Her husband—winded—remained some distance below with a second porter and coolie, and took pictures of Nun Kun.

The Workmans wound up their Far Eastern adventures by spending two summers in the ice wilds of Eastern Karakoram.

It all began back in Worcester, Massachusetts, where Fanny was born on January 8, 1859, the daughter of Alexander Hamilton Bullock, a former governor of Massachusetts. By the time she and Doctor Workman were married in 1881, Fanny had scaled peaks in the White Mountains, among the highest in the eastern part of the United States. But these were midget peaks compared with the mighty peaks of the Alps and the much mightier peaks of the Himalayas she was to scale later.

Until her husband suffered from a lung ailment, and gave up his practice of medicine eight years after their marriage, Fanny had no serious thought of leaving behind her friends and relatives in Worcester in exchange for travel and exploration. When they set out for faraway places, her one ambition in life was to help William recover his health. In that she succeeded, too!

Before their adventures were over, she had been honored by the French Alpine Club with the Grand Medaille for scaling the highest peaks in the Alps, 15,781-foot-high Mont Blanc, the Matterhorn, and the treacherous Jûngfrau. She was the first American woman ever to lecture at the Sorbonne. She gave lectures at the Appalachian Mountain Club of Boston, and the Alpine and Camera clubs of London. She wrote books of travel, geography, and geological research in collaboration with her scholarly husband.

Best of all, the Workmans turned a marriage which early seemed doomed to defeat, because of William's poor health, into a lengthy honeymoon.

For in spite of many perils, thieving natives, and mutinous coolies who deserted them at the most inconvenient times; in spite of setbacks that would have maddened many couples, they never regretted their decision to make the Himalayas their play- and work-ground for many years. They would return to Worcester only long enough to lecture in Boston and plan other expeditions.

Mountaineering in the Himalayas, Fanny and William found, was quite different from mountaineering in Switzerland and in the Tyrol. In the Himalayas, there were no villages and hotels within a few hours distance of the summits, no shelter huts where a climber might break the journey and get a good night's sleep, no cheerful experienced guides to render immediate aid.

It was a wild, fascinating country where mountaineers had to set out before dawn, fully provided with mountain and camp gear that had come from great distances. The semicivilized villages were far apart. There were savage and trackless wastes surrounding the inscrutable giant mountains they would conquer. They had to brave weariness, cold winds blowing as much as eighty miles an hour; wet, blinding snow; wide changes in temperature within a single day; the dizzying, dulling effects of high altitude without then-unheard-of oxygen equipment.

Later, Fanny Workman wrote: "It has been asserted that, aside from their altitude, the Himalayas are very easy mountains to ascend. Let no one cherish this delusion. Let no one suppose that the world's vastest mountain chain is fashioned on any such mild scheme as this. In the Himalayas are mountains of all kinds and sizes. Some can be ascended. Many more probably never will be by any creature without wings. There are perpendicular walls towering thousands of feet above the valleys, precipices descending into abysses which sunlight never penetrates, pointed spires and aiguilles piercing the loftiest clouds, so sharp they scorn the snow mantle nature would throw around them. These are the Matterhorns, the Grepous, and Funfinger many times magnified, vast fields of snow arêtes and domes of snow crowning inaccessible rock massifs.

"The mountain flanks are constantly scored by avalanches of snow and rock, which thunder down at all hours of the day. Immense landslides are frequent. They fill valleys and dam back the water from the melting snow, which later bursts the unstable barrier thus formed, and tears downward, a living mass of water, mud and rock, with terrific force, carrying all before it and spreading devastation and ruin in its path. Against these, as well as driving winds and dangers of glaciers with their enormous crevasses, a mountaineer must be constantly on guard."

On their first expedition to the Himalayas, the Workmans camped in tents erected in village graveyards or sometimes even on the roof of a native shack. There was no privacy. Dirty, curious villagers gaped at them day and night. Sleep was hard to come by because of the cries of harsh cackling voices, ear-splitting coughs, howls of wild leopards in the night, and the general noise and confusion. Eventually they selected camping sites on the outskirts of a village, or some distance away. Though these were not always comfortable or safe from wild animals, at least there was some degree of privacy.

As the spell of the Himalayas wove its magic on the Workmans, they began to understand why the men of this hill country worshiped those great temples of nature, and peopled their icy mountains and dells with imaginary deities.

But inspiring though the mountain heights were, with tiny white-flowered edelweiss similar to that found in the Alps surprising them suddenly in rock crevasses, the natives seldom measured up to the country's grandeur and beauty.

The first *khansamah* (cook) they engaged, a Kashmiri,

turned out to be an enigmatic character. He came bringing high recommendation. Encouraged by this, the Workmans gave him several rupees. When, at the end of the week, they asked for an accounting, he replied in English: "Yes, thank you." When asked if he was buying provisions on credit, he answered a polite "No." Two weeks later, however, he presented a bill for food many times greater than the sum advanced him. It was itemized for each day, written in good English hand by one of the hangers-on at the bazaar in Srinagar. The items bore little relation to what was furnished, and were charged at from three to six times the cost of such articles in the bazaar. Called on to explain, the cook merely said: "Yes, thank you." They soon discovered this phrase and "No" were the extent of his English vocabulary. Still, since he was a fairly good cook, and the Workmans discovered they could do no better, they paid the bill and said nothing. In time, they learned to cope with their devious Kashmiri cook, pruning the account without offending his dignity. So satisfied was he with his tactful employers that he returned to serve them the following year. On another expedition, the cook at times stole the food of the porters, and always gave them such skimpy rations that they often went to bed hungry. This time Fanny decided to dispense with his services, and let the porters fend for themselves in the culinary line.

Another of their early acquisitions was a Leh interpreter who spoke English and Nubra dialect. Since, at first, Fanny and William spoke only a little Hindustani, the official language, and no native dialects at all, they were glad to get him.

He was a sly cunning Madrassi, married to the daughter of a petty official, and went by the Christian name of "Mr. Paul." "Mr. Paul," the Workmans soon found out, had a genius for extorting high wages. He insisted he needed money for two ponies to carry himself and his luggage, as well as money for a new suit of clothing. Although his last employer had provided him with a new suit, he turned up for his duties in destitute condition. Soon after the Workmans supplied him with cash, however, he appeared in white Ellwood topie, a tweed riding coat with knickerbockers, garters, English boots with pointed toes, and an English riding whip. He rode on a Nubran pony, and behind came another pony bearing his luggage. Though Fanny Workman was greatly amused at "Mr. Paul's" ostentation, he turned out to be a good investment. Not only was he an excellent interpreter, but the natives regarded the Workman caravan with great respect, thanks to the elegant "Mr. Paul." He was, however, eventually dispensed with when Fanny and William became more familiar with the native tongues.

In their first year of exploring and mountain climbing in the Himalayas, the Workmans made the ascent of Mahadeo peak, 13,084 feet high. This, however, was a puny peak compared with the 26,660-foot Nanga Parbat, which towered above it, and others to the northwest, looking down on the Vale of Kashmir and the winding Jhelum River.

It took only three days to make the Mahadeo ascent, but the Workmans had the thrill of being probably the first people in the world to leave their calling cards there in a glass jar, before descending to Shalimar Bagh, then returning to Srinagar.

From Srinagar they journeyed to Leh, about 250 miles away. They reached this capital of Ladakh late in June, in time for the religious festival, or miracle play, which took place at the Buddhist monastery, twenty-five miles east. The interesting, fantastic ceremonies they saw there reminded them, much to their surprise, of rites seen in formal, ritualistic Christian churches.

In 1892, Sir Martin Conway, on a Karakoram journey, first visited the Hispar region. He made a quick survey of the main stream, but did not investigate its many long tributaries. The Workmans decided to take up where he left off.

Between 1900 and 1904, they began a detailed survey of the whole region, making careful glacial studies, observing weather and altitude conditions. In order to find good points of observation, they ascended as many nearby peaks as they could, but climbing mountains merely as stunts seemed not nearly as important to them as accurately investigating and mapping this fantastic country.

Before they could begin a new expedition, it was necessary to win the approval of the native ruler of Nagar. For it was at Nagar they would set out to reach the Hispar Glacier before beginning the three-hundred-mile foot and horse journey through valleys and passes.

The Indian rajah, slim, fair-skinned, and handsome, was fond of European clothes, just as "Mr. Paul" had been. He appeared in an English coat, wearing patent leather boots, and immediately presented Fanny with a sheep and a large ball of ghee, or clarified butter. She in turn gave his young princess a silk scarf, mirrors and amulets.

The rajah tried to discourage Fanny from going on so perilous a journey, telling her the "mountain gods" would disapprove. When she insisted on going, he agreed to furnish sixty or seventy coolies to carry loads on the glaciers. He also said he would change them every two weeks with relief coolies sent up from Nagar. (It proved to be an expensive expedition for the Workmans, for, besides wages, they were obliged to feed each coolie two pounds of rice or flour daily, and purchase at usury rates thirty sheep and twelve goats for camp use.)

When the "bargain" was completed, the rajah clapped his hands. Soon a court orchestra appeared, playing weird-sounding music on strange stringed instruments. Next a band of Nagaris rushed in, and began a hectic war dance, to the accompaniment of shawms and tom-toms. When the ceremony was over, the rajah smiled at Fanny Workman and her husband, offering them his undying friendship. "But after some years of Asiatic travel," said Fanny, "we know how much value to attach to the honeyed words of an Oriental."

Though Fanny and William Workman did not break any mountain-climbing records at Hispar, Fanny did climb its highest peak, between fifteen and twenty thousand feet. As a result, she was laid up for a time with fever and severe chest pains. This, however, did not keep her and her husband from going on with their original long-term plans. That summer, and for four summers afterwards, the Workmans were absorbed with their explorations of the Biafo Glacier, and many others. They went to parts of the Himalayas where no humans—only leopards—had gone before. They, their German topographer, and Zurbriggen, their Italian guide, accompanied by baggage train, coolies, goats, sheep, and yaks, explored sources, formations, and movements of glaciers, and recorded altitudes of many a wind-swept mountain peak.

For weeks at a time, the Workmans, with climbing ropes, ice-picks, thermometers, cameras, and other scientific equipment of the day, camped at altitudes above fifteen thousand feet. They succeeded in reaching the source of the great Chogo Lungma Glacier, thirty-one miles long, and never before ascended. They traversed vast areas never before visited, discovered peaks and glaciers no map had ever indicated. One king of the snow peaks they christened Mount Bullock-Workman, and erecting a large cairn of rocks on its summit, left a record of their expedition's doings.

By the year 1906, Fanny Bullock Workman and William were experienced and tough enough as Himalayan mountain climbers to undertake their most ambitious and dangerous adventure.

»»

For some years, while passing through the Suru Valley in eastern Kashmir, Fanny and her husband had been struck by the magnificence of the Nun Kun Range. No snow peaks in the Himalayas fascinated them as much. Its highest peaks reached far through the clear evening sky, surrounded by perfect sheer rock aiguilles flecked with snow, and tinted with red afterglow. Nun Kun seemed to bring heaven closer. No matter what other ranges they saw, they could not forget the fairy-like enticement of Nun Kun.

In the spring of 1906, when they decided to make the daring climb up the Nun Kun Range, the natives of Srinagar shook their heads. Although the coolies in the Suru Valley were starving because of crop failures, they doubted if any would accompany the Workmans.

"Why not?" Fanny asked.

"Nun Kun is the abode of the most sacred mountain gods," said a native. "It is not for human beings to climb. It is too high, too dangerous!"

The others nodded. Nevertheless, Fanny and William Workman went ahead with their plans. They recruited Cyprien Savoye, one of the best guides from Cournsajeur, and six experienced Italian porters.

When Fanny asked them what they thought of the native "myths," Cyprien Savoye shrugged, but one of the porters put in, "Perhaps there is something to it. Let us try another range."

"No," said Fanny Workman. "Let us try Nun Kun."

By May, 1906, the expedition was ready to start. Reluctantly, the starving coolies agreed to go if they would be provided with eight weeks of meal and rice for the forbidden journey. This amounted to 16,000 pounds. The provisions, along with necessary tinned food, were sent on to Suru, a twelve-days' march from Srinagar, along with the caravan of 245 coolies, under the leadership of the Workmans' English agent. Before they reached Suru 100 coolies deserted at the first high pass they came to, carrying off what provisions they could steal and leaving the rest strewn on the path. Because of this shortage of coolies, it took the agent three weeks, making short double marches each day, to arrive at Suru. All this Fanny and William Workman discovered when they reached Suru.

It was the end of June before they left this base for upper Suru Valley. Fanny wore an English cap, a heavy tweed suit with medium-length skirt. Her bearded husband wore a wide-brimmed hat, tweed jacket and trousers. Both wore bright, striped wool stockings, mountain boots, and carried walking staffs. The porters were supplied with climbing ropes, ice pikes, and other necessary equipment. Of course they brought tents and sleeping bags. With their sixty remaining coolies, their guide and porters, 25 sheep, and 16 goats, they headed for Shafat Valley leading to the Shafat Glacier, the northern approach to Nun Kun's highest peaks.

What should have been a two-days' journey from Suru village was an exhausting, lengthy ordeal. For this year, the raging, bridgeless Suru River was so swollen by melting glaciers that it was almost impossible to ford. Three times they tried and failed. Even when they finally succeeded in making it to the opposite shore, and laboriously went on until they came to the entrance of Shafat Valley, the natives were restive. So were some of the Italian porters.

These were no Alpine peaks they were asked to climb, grumbled the Europeans. These were giant foreign peaks with the curse of strange gods on them!

"Nonsense," said Fanny Workman, as she fought off their superstitions. Nonetheless, she had some misgivings, and asked her husband for support.

"Of course we'll go on if you insist, Fanny," he told her.

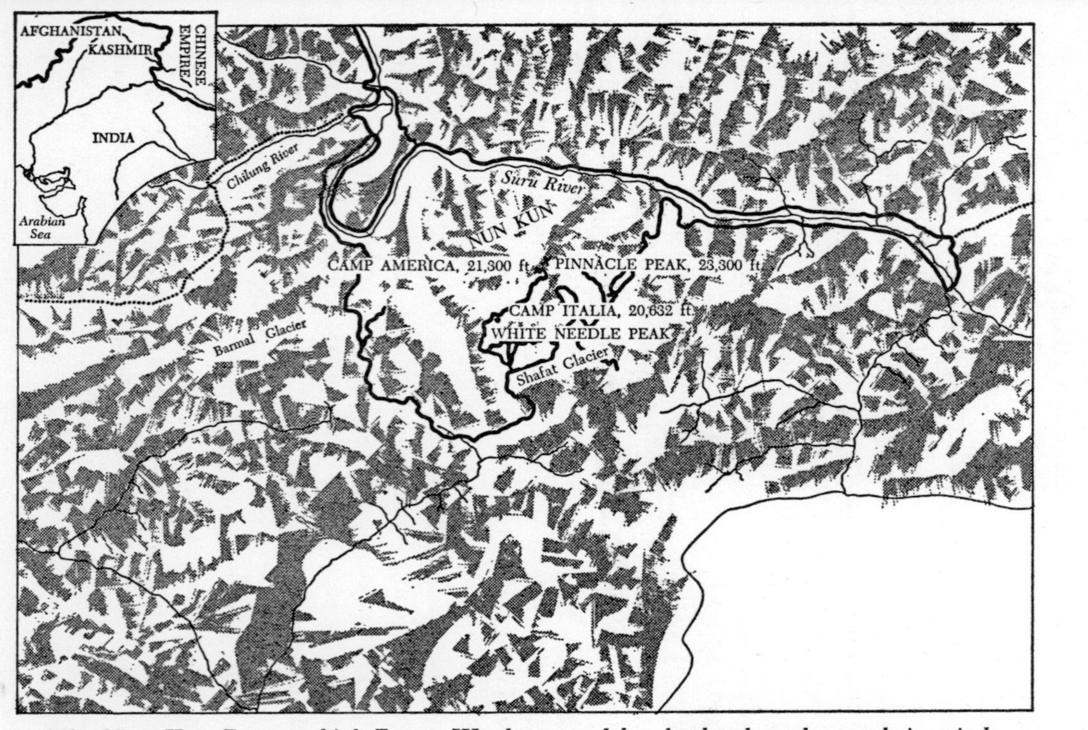

The Nun Kun Range which Fanny Workman and her husband made up their minds to climb. They couldn't forget its magnificence, which had struck them while they were passing through the Suru Valley in eastern Kashmir.

So they went on, defying the foreign mountain gods.

When finally they made their base camp at 15,100 feet, far up the Shafat Glacier, Fanny stood on the rough spur of the lower Nun Kun, staring up at the mighty ice falls and saddles of the towering massif. Here no human beings had ever dared to go before. For a moment, the exhilaration of this thought made her yearn to dash up the mountainside, and plant a flagstaff at its very top. But she knew that neither she nor her husband would be satisfied merely with climbing one of the mightiest Himalayan peaks. Much as Nun Kun lured them, they would follow their usual method of work: study the glaciers as they went along, make detailed observations, and measure as accurately as they could all gaps and projections. Moreover, they would set their tents at high altitudes and remain at each long enough to observe the effects of wind pressure—which sometimes reached eighty miles an hour —and the effects of rarefied air especially on their European porters. Of course, the already murmuring coolies would probably turn tail and not take part in the bold experiment.

The Workmans' plans went along as they had hoped. Leaving the coolies in this lower camp, six porters went on ahead, carrying the heavy camp equipment. Fanny, her husband, and the guide, went with them.

Thanks to the fact the porters did their own cooking now, none of the group went hungry as porters in the past had done, when the thieving Kashmiri cook was in charge. After a hard day aloft, a large saucepan of soup would be set to steaming over a stone fireplace carved out by nature; or a half sheep be placed on a spit to roast. On many a bleak mountain ledge, the Workmans and their aides enjoyed a home-cooked dinner.

For one week they stayed on in the upper part of the Shafat Glacier and another east ice fall, investigating every detail. Then they climbed the lower peaks to orient themselves, measuring and mapping them as well as they could.

Since the weather had been fine so far they decided to establish camp farther up. From a projection just above the base camp they could spy the highest Nun Kun peak, but other lofty summits were shut off from sight by lesser mountains and a great ice wall which must be passed before they could reach the pinnacle of their dreams.

The guide Savoye and two porters made preliminary inspection. So favorably impressed were they with what they found, it was decided to send four porters ahead with light camp kit and establish a new base. Then, if the reluctant coolies could be inveigled into climbing higher, the porters would push on alone from the new base, leaving tents and provisions. After a scouting expedition, they would rejoin the rest.

Fanny and William Workman gave them a few days' start. Then, one clear morning, they left with the guide, remaining porters and fourteen fearful coolies. The rest refused to budge from the lower base.

Over great moraine ridges Fanny and the others climbed; through icy glacial torrents they waded. At last, they approached the snowy Himalayan peaks. Here, as they ascended the slippery snowslopes, keeping close together on the rope harnesses, they came on interesting stretches of "Penitent Snows," sometimes found in the Andes. But this was the first time the Workmans had seen the spectacle in the Himalayas. They were small corrugated ice-pinnacles, from one foot to three feet high. With combs of snow turning downward, they gave the appearance of groups of penitent monks, hence the name.

By one P.M. they came to a snow hollow beside a few rocks. The coolies lit fires on the flimsy base and helped cook the food. Here, camping on snow at 17,657 feet, they stayed the night. This was the last good sleep Fanny and William Workman were to have in many a night.

The next day's climb was a hard precarious one over walls of ice, up sharp, wind-swept inclines slashed by great crevices. At first, the coolies marched bravely, but, even with the encouragement of the porters and guide, they threatened to turn back, as the dangers increased. The "mountain gods" would be offended if they went farther!

However, later in the afternoon, having made it alive to some high snow *seracs*, they shook themselves out of their stupors and shouted gleefully. For farther up on a solitary snow slope could be seen a fire, and two tiny shelter tents.

Looking through a Zeiss glass, Fanny Workman saw the three small figures of the porters, descending an ice wall high above their tents. They seemed like frail dark specks against the white magnitude of Nun Kun.

Ice, wind, and snow—ice, wind, and snow! Everywhere, steep slippery inclines from which, in a moment, one might be hurled to instant oblivion! For several days they pushed on like robots. Now, breathless from high altitude, they finally reached the tents of the three porters. They were exhausted and panting; their lips parched; their chests throbbing with pain, but they had made this fearsome, awe-inspiring site, 19,900 feet high, according to careful measurements. The Workmans called it "White Needle Camp," because of a tall white aiguille, towering on the left, and flanked by an ice wall which appeared to be at least 700 feet high. This perilous wall had to be scaled before the enigma of Nun Kun could be confronted.

Now, most of the coolies, worn out and terrified, lay prostrate in the snow. Some were suffering violently from mountain sickness. But two hardy natives and a tent servant offered to stay on and carry loads the next day. The others, when able to stand up again, were sent down to the lower camp.

After warm nourishing soup, the Workmans and party tried to get some much needed sleep, but at this bivouac, five hundred and fifty feet higher than their last highest camp, they found it more and more painful to breathe. It took all one's power of will to exercise the lungs in this diminished atmosphere. Many times during that night, Fanny tossed in her sleeping bag, fearful not so much that she would suffocate as that her husband, who had once suffered from weak lungs, could not endure this rarefied altitude. She even began to feel that perhaps the "mountain gods" were in league to destroy them. They lived through the dreadful night and, having come this far, they determined not to turn back, though none in the party had slept a wink.

For three days they climbed, dazed from lack of sleep and lack of oxygen, but dedicated to conquering the ice wall. All the porters bore loads of at least forty pounds.

The magnitude of Nun Kun now seemed more unattainable than ever. In two roped caravans, the party marched. No word was spoken on the lines except when one of the porters gasped out, "Halt!" Each hour seemed more unbearable than the last, for now they were on a perpendicular face of a slope, constantly forced to drive in ice axes and spiked boots so that they would not be hurled, by driving winds, into the icy abyss below. The yawning blue chasm fluted with snow ruffles seemed to lure one to lose balance and consciousness, and fall into its merciless depths.

Despite shortness of breath, a constant battle against the elements and against dizziness, they ascended several hundred feet, determined more than ever to try an ascending traverse of the wall. Now it seemed as if the "mountain gods" were daring them to go higher.

Once Fanny Workman's eyes were lured toward the great Shafat Glacier which lay in shadow, that smooth snowsheet thousands of feet beneath. Then, in order to retain consciousness, she resolutely lifted her gaze to the hills, and saw wave after wave of snow mountains. As early sun darted across them, the beautiful ranges of Zanskar turned mauve and ruby. Behind them rose only an unending wall. The outer snow coating of this wall was fast melting. It was high time they reached more secure footing.

Now, as the guide Savoye shortened each halt to a few seconds, he led stoically on. Fanny could hear her own hoarse breathing, and that of her husband and the others. At last, they came to a projecting snow buttress. Savoye, held fast by two porters, carved out a short, straight staircase. Then all, with infinite care, mounted this. To their welcome surprise, they found themselves once more on firm snow, and were able to make their way over slight rising slopes now with greater ease. They paused to rest their overtaxed lungs and worn-out bodies. At last, slightly rested, they advanced again. As they did so—slowly and carefully—Fanny Workman saw stretching before her a never-to-be forgotten sight of the magic world of the Himalayas. Never before had she seen such magnificence as that of the Nun Kun snow lake or high basin now unfolding.

She saw a plateau, at least one and a half by three miles, whose existence none had even suspected. Except by coming the precarious way they had come, Nun Kun was unapproachable on all sides. It rose and fell in dazzling white billows. Above, piercing the sky like bright flashing swords, loomed its highest peaks, with the aiguilles she and her husband had often seen below from the valley. The peaks appeared to be much lower from the basin, of course, than when they had been standing far down in the valley. For they were now nearing the end of their perilous journey up Nun Kun. That afternoon, after climbing without rest for three days, they made camp at 20,632 feet, naming the site "Camp Italia" in honor of the native land of their guide and porters.

The Workmans spent the afternoon studying the glacial outlets to the basin, in making observations, and in deciding which summit they would try to scale. After a thorough reconnaissance, they chose the second highest peak of Nun Kun, about 150 feet lower than the mightiest. With the porters' heavy loads, and with one of the Italians desperately ill from altitude, they could not risk staying much longer at such dizzy heights as they had now reached.

They spent another cold, insomnia-racked night. Before sunup, the Workmans, their guide, and three of the porters were on their way again, bringing as little camp equipment as possible. Climbing up and down snow hillocks, they reached a so-called plateau at a higher altitude; here the snow was soft and in very bad condition. A mist now came in. By the time the Workman tents were pitched, a snowstorm was beginning. As the guide and the three porters had left their own tents, clothing, and food at "Camp Italia," and could not stay here without returning for them, it was decided they would go back for them. If possible, they would return by sunset. Otherwise, Fanny and William Workman would remain alone until the following day.

As Fanny saw the others disappear in the deep fog, a feeling of dreadful isolation came over her. She and William busied themselves with their instruments. By careful measurement, they found that this base was at an altitude of 21,300 feet.

They called it "Camp America," and took consolation in knowing it was the highest camp in the Himalayas ever made by explorers; the highest measured point at which mountaineers had ever spent a night.

By two o'clock in the afternoon, the snow stopped. Through the mist, the sun shone faintly, producing a sickening heat, even at this high altitude. They wrapped their heads in wet towels. With their black bulb thermometer, they observed that the temperature was 193 degrees F. By four P.M., it had gone down to 140 degrees. Soon after sunset, the temperature dropped. By seven P.M. their glass stood at zero; later that night, it registered four below. Thus, since pitching camp, they had endured variations of temperature of 197 degrees!

It was late when, fortified by soup prepared over a small Swedish stove, they climbed into their eider sleeping sacks. Exhausted though they both were, no sleep came to either. The hours seemed endless. They lay there, gasping for breath.

"We shouldn't have come, should we?" Fanny asked chokingly. "Maybe the natives are right."

Her husband, struggling hard to breathe, made no reply.

At daybreak, when they heard the click of ice axes, their spirits revived. Then Savoye and two porters trudged toward them, icicles hanging from their hair and moustaches.

Fanny turned with forced effort and little strength to get coffee for the group before starting the upward climb again. The stove, too, suffered from lack of oxygen, and seemed to take hours to light. At last, fortified by hot coffee, they managed to struggle into their frozen boots. Though they had little appetite for food now, they packed up some congealed meat, biscuits, and chocolate, and were on their way.

Now nerve power alone seemed to keep them going, as hour after hour they climbed the sharpest slopes. At several points, gruesome pinnacled ice falls made further ascent impossible. Savoye and the two porters worked their axes with skillful, amazing energy, in spite of the terrible difficulties. Again and again they hacked and chopped out the mountain side.

At 22,720 feet, they carved out some hollows in the snow, and all sat down for a scanty meal, but they felt nauseated. Now they decided to change their route and follow a sharp rock arête, almost snowless, with a precipice dropping into space on its outer side. Although highly dangerous, it was the one way to go.

But only Fanny Bullock Workman, her guide, and one porter, were to continue this ascent! Doctor Workman, suffering from the effects of high altitude more than he liked to admit, finally agreed to stay here with another porter and coolie, and, if heavy clouds did not interfere, take pictures of Nun Kun.

Later, Fanny was to say that chivalry impelled her husband to remain some distance below—that he wanted "his Fanny" to take the family bows for making it to the very top of Nun Kun's second highest peak. And perhaps this was so.

Fanny Bullock Workman recalled little of the next hour and a half. Every ounce of energy left was now focused on leaping from crag to crag, for difficult rock climbing at over 22,000 feet was a hundred times harder than climbing on snow. Every three minutes or so, Savoye called, "Halt." They wet their parched lips, and went doggedly on.

One scene, however, Fanny would always remember: pausing once on this rock pinnacle sharper than the Matterhorn and thousands of feet higher than Mont Blanc, she happened to glance to her right. As she did so, her eye fell on a deathly void far below, in which other summits lifted their pigmy tops. From their flanks, glaciers wove their way toward green valleys now lost in haze. At this view there was no nearby higher peak to offer moral support. This precipice seemed to overhang the whole world. There was nothing to look up to.

"To one affected with vertigo," she was to recall, "the sight would have been impossible, but fortunately, I was not affected that way."

Then, the miracle was accomplished. They reached the top and were in the company now of the "mountain gods."

Far below lay the vast thinly populated mountain world of the Middle Himalayas—spreading out on three sides in snow waves like an arctic floe. To the southwest, very slightly above them now, rose the highest peak, wrapped in cloud. A cold driving wind lashed at Fanny; the lack of oxygen made her overtaxed lungs scream for relief.

But she stood her ground for a few minutes. She carefully

measured the altitude, not believing what she read at first. To reassure herself, she let Savoye take a reading. There was no doubt about it. The altitude was 23,300 feet! This was the highest altitude ever reached by any mountain climber to date!

Before starting down, Fanny Workman named the mountain top "Pinnacle Peak," and felt as if she must have really reached the abode of the "mountain gods."

As they rejoined the others below, there was little time to celebrate, however, for descending the Himalayas in the afternoon was extremely risky. They must start at once, for it was past noon. Already the sun's heat was so penetrating, they greatly feared an avalanche as they picked their way down the sharp incline of "Pinnacle Peak." At each wary step, they sank through onto ice. Finally, at seven P.M. they arrived at "Camp America."

"We felt like thanking the mountain gods for letting us through so easily," said Fanny Workman.

But their ordeal was not yet over. As usual, they could not sleep that night. The cold was unbearable, for, although only six degrees F.—by no means a low temperature—they were greatly weakened by loss of sleep in past nights, and want of oxygen. In this condition, they suffered more, said Fanny, than an arctic explorer in weather forty degrees below zero, but at low altitude.

Next day, crossing the plateau, they descended to "White Needle Camp," and spent their last sleepless night there.

They were up early, however, and traveled well into the night. When they reached base camp, they found servants preparing the fatted sheep for their arrival, while the lower slopes of Nun Kun teamed with coolies, eager to bring down the camp equipment.

For now they regarded Fanny Bullock Workman as an approved member of the deity!

Fanny, her husband, and their aides spent the better part of two days sleeping. By the end of the third day—elated by their most successful mountain climb—they felt in excellent health and spirits.

As a result of this brave adventure, Fanny Workman and her husband dispelled some of the superstitions which had haunted the natives. They made the task of mountain climbing in the Himalayas easier for others who would follow them.

They demonstrated that European porters were in some ways better than native coolies, for even at high altitudes they had carried loads of from thirty to forty pounds. On moderate inclines above the height of 22,000 feet, some might succeed, while others would surely give out. And there seemed no way of telling in advance which people could stand the strain. For, to their astonishment, one of those who had suffered most from mountain sickness at great heights was their strongest porter.

The greatest menaces to mountain climbing in the Himalayas, they found, were migraine, severe nausea, lack of appetite, lassitude, and general debility. Yet only one of the Europeans suffered so much as not to be able to carry out daily tasks.

The body was certainly under great strain above the height of 20,000 feet, and insomnia was bound to occur. Indeed, some of the symptoms increased, rather than decreased, the longer one remained at great heights.

"I believe that when the highest peaks of the Himalayas are seriously attacked," Fanny Workman said in one of her lectures, "more will fail through sleeplessness and its effects than any other cause. For it is the true mother of all altitude symptoms and more to be dreaded, particularly on Mount Everest, than mountain sickness."

Though others—with better mountain climbing equipment and maps—have now surpassed the mountain-climbing record set by Fanny Bullock Workman and her husband back in 1906, no mountain climbers, men or women, ever surpassed them in pioneer daring and courage.

Following the death of her husband, Fanny spent the latter part of her life in France. She died in Cannes at the age of sixty-six, on January 22, 1925, honored in her lifetime by her husband and by many countries. She is still remembered as the Himalayas' bravest woman explorer.

KATHLEEN M. KENYON

To most people, the dump heap known as Old Jericho seemed unimpressive on this early spring morning in 1952. It was a familiar blight on the landscape, lying on the outskirts of the modern Near East town of Jericho of more than 41,000 inhabitants. In this sun-baked Jordan Valley of dates, bananas, oranges, and figs, the unfinished Greek monastery on the Mount of Temptations, not far away, was much more eye-catching. So were the Latin chapel, Russian hospice, and several tourist hotels.

Certainly, the shabbily dressed Arab women from surrounding camps seemed unaware of its existence. They stood near the old mill buildings at the foot of the high mound, chatting and laughing together as they drew water from Jericho's gushing spring—just as women had been doing for ages past.

Kathleen Kenyon, a vital-looking English woman clad in trim work blouse and skirt, stood apart from the group, gazing up at the mound with suppressed excitement. From time to time, she jotted down notes on a small pad. Her eyes, framed by a short brownish-gray bob, were intensely alive as she surveyed the seventy-foot high, oval-shaped heap which sprawled over at least eight acres of gray rubbly soil.

As an explorer of the past—an archaeologist—her keen glances detected hidden meanings in every indentation and ridge up there. She examined the road cut into the eastern edge—the road which led north up the west side of the Jordan Valley toward Jerusalem, seventeen miles away. Obviously the cut in the road had distorted the original shape of the mound. She hoped not too much treasure of the past had been sealed up in this way. For this site, set in a deep valley far below sea level, between the famed Sea of Galilee, where Jesus once walked, and the Dead Sea, was the ancient city of Jericho. It was because of its strategic location and excellent spring watering that it first became an artery of travel and an important town.

The records of centuries seemed to live and breathe all around Kathleen Kenyon. Here, at Jericho, Joshua and the Israelites, after a miraculous crossing of the Jordan River, marched around the Canaanites' city, blowing their horns. Seven times, the story went. Then, as they let out a mighty shout, the wall of Jericho came tumbling down! She smiled, remembering how thrilled she had been in childhood, back in an English manor house, as she listened to this and other Bible stories about Jericho. She was very young, the daughter of Sir Frederic Kenyon, and had no doubts in those days that horns and shouts could make a wall come tumbling down.

Even later, when she went away to St. Paul's School for girls and then to Somerville College, England, she was still intrigued by this town of Jericho. So many times it was mentioned in the Bible. Here Elisha cured the poisonous waters of its spring on one occasion. In the New Testament, Jericho was linked with the blind Bartimeus, the publican Zacchaeus, and the Good Samaritan. Herod made Jericho his winter residence, living in pomp and dying here.

Now, at forty-six, a veteran archaeologist of field expeditions, beginning in 1929 at Southern Rhodesia, then going on to Verulamium, Samaria, Leicester, Viroconium-Bath, and other historical sites in England and elsewhere, she had come to Jericho to mastermind a limited digging out of the historic city.

Buried in this ugly mound, she knew, were many fascinating mysteries. In spite of archaeological peckings-away here, beginning a hundred years ago, only the surface of Jericho's story had been scratched. The last exploration had been made by Professor Garstang of Liverpool University twenty-six years before, and some of his findings were now in dispute. The British School of Archaeology in Jerusalem assigned Kathleen Kenyon to go to Jericho and re-examine the Joshua era, using new techniques for removal of soil and recording layers. She was to re-evaluate the period through studying "finds," such as pottery, flint, skeletons, and defense structures.

Kathleen Kenyon knew how much hard, painstaking work, tedium, and frustration, as well as teamwork and scientific know-how, went into the digging out of a ruin. She knew, too, that high exciting moments lay ahead for her in her search to find out how people lived long ago, traced from fragmentary records left behind. What they ate, wore, their customs of burial, what their houses were like—these were among the things she wanted to learn. For an archaeologist is not only an explorer of the past, but a detective unraveling a mystery story. As in a mystery story, one clue led to another. Sometimes one followed false clues, had to go back and rearrange the pieces of the puzzle. As in a mystery story, the outcome could be most surprising.

As Kathleen Kenyon went about making final preparations for her first season, she had no idea, however, just how surprising the outcome of her Jericho story would be. She had no idea that, in her six years here, she would do more than mastermind a limited digging out of the Joshua era. She would go much farther in her findings and, in so doing, make one of the most astounding discoveries in archaeological history.

Kathleen Kenyon's first season at Jericho began with many setbacks and delays. The equipment she begged and borrowed from the British School of Archaeology in Jerusalem was three weeks late in arriving. She and her international staff—some of them specialists in their fields, some of them students—soon set up Spartan headquarters in the old mill buildings and in tents set up in a banana grove at the foot of the *tell.* There was not enough bedding to go round, and in spite of warm days, the desert nights were cold. The darkroom where photographs were developed, and the rooms for sorting, labeling, and stacking finds from the Jericho diggings, were cramped. There just wasn't enough living and working space.

There wasn't enough of anything excepting unemployed Arab laborers who clamored for jobs. In her seasons at Jericho, Kathleen Kenyon hired between 120 and 250 Arab workers to do the hard digging. They had to be very closely supervised. Though they proved more bother than help at first—they could not understand why digging holes in the ground had to be done with such precision—they soon took pride in working for this "odd" English lady. They formed a "father-and-son" work guild to keep intruders from getting their seasonal work away from them. Even when they became expert at the diggings, they could never understand why Kathleen Kenyon got so excited about finding bits of broken pottery or an ancient ant-eaten mat. As for crawling right into the tombs with the dead—as if she enjoyed it!—each time she did that, they sent a quick prayer to Allah to keep a curse away from the English lady and themselves.

The Kenyon field expedition was far behind schedule in starting the first excavations, and because the season for work was short—from February to April in this land where scorching summer heat came early—Kathleen and her staff had to work long hours, sometimes far into the night.

In spite of agonizing delays, however, they finally began a limited sounding at the *tell* where Professor Garstang left off his diggings years ago. For each archaeologist begins with the findings of the archaeologist who has been there before. Then, with more modern techniques, the old findings are reassessed, and one goes on from there. Twenty-six years had passed since the professor worked at Jericho. Besides the inroads which time, weather, and scavengers had made, less care had been taken by past archaeologists in the matter of dirt removal. They dug straight deep shafts, and in their hurry to examine a rich find, mixed together soil and finds from differing levels and periods.

The first job was carefully to shift the dumps left behind, a supervisor recording a description of the soil, and putting all finds in a labeled container for future examination. Then a small area was marked out in a square to the south of the *tell* and careful excavation began there. The Arab laborers, with Kathleen and other staff members attending very closely, tenderly cut through the slope of the *tell* in order to expose a fresh, large section of lower levels of the city and be able to study the series relating to the Joshua era.

This painstaking method of digging was used by Kathleen

Kenyon in all future excavations of other sites at Jericho. Though time-consuming and requiring great skill and knowledge, it brought far better results than did the old haphazard diggings. So did the patient method of sorting and labeling the finds, with the aid of an anthropologist in the field, as soon as possible after they were uncovered. At the end of each day, the finds were then taken to the dig headquarters. The next day they were washed, marked, and tied up in bags or boxes, and stored for more careful screening and recording.

In addition, a draftsman and photographer were on the spot to make visual records of each site as soon as uncovered. Thus Kathleen Kenyon could study at leisure different levels of the town, different types of structures, different kinds of pottery, figurines, et cetera, and especially different types of burials. For the way people were buried told a great deal about their lives and era.

Because of this tortoise-like method of digging, the exploration of the cemetery areas—a most important phase of archaeological exploration—had scarcely begun when the season was almost over. Yet already Kathleen Kenyon and her co-workers were coming upon clues beginning to reveal a bigger story than they had come for.

Professor Garstang had traced a double line of upper-level wall which he attributed to the final stage of the Bronze Age. He believed its ruin was caused by Joshua's attack, but due to excavations at other Near East sites, scholars now disputed the era he set for Joshua's entrance into Palestine. They placed the dates variously as 1400 B.C. and 1260 B.C.

Kathleen Kenyon began to find contradictions. She soon found evidence of the wall's destruction by earthquake and fire. The bricks of the wall fell outwards, for one thing, and were badly scorched on the inner side. Though Joshua might have regarded such destruction as providential, a more detailed examination of the debris showed the wall belonged to an earlier period than either the professor or scholars had given. But it was to be many seasons of checking and rechecking evidence before Kathleen Kenyon was to make a wary estimate that the "Joshua" wall belonged to the third quarter of the fourteenth century B.C., and so was in ruins at the time ascribed to Joshua's entrance into Palestine.

Meanwhile, she was finding traces of earlier defenses on lower levels, suggesting collapses due entirely to natural decay. With each collapse of the level, the *tell* rose, so each defense was formed on an earlier one. Even during her first season, she came upon fragmentary evidence in the way of pottery, figurines, and building structures that pointed to more than one Jericho city—some very old.

The most startling "find" of the 1952 season in this direction came at the close of the season, when Kathleen Kenyon uncovered the remains of an ancient shrine on a lower level. It was a large rectangular room twenty-five feet by about twenty feet, with stone pillars set in altar niches at either end. In the center of the room was a small, skillfully made stone basin, covered by highly burnished plaster, as were the floors and walls. The basin was slightly scorched. It had obviously been used for sacrificial rites, for later she found charred human and animal remains under foundation stones. On the same site were found fertility figurines and a small figure of a mother-goddess.

Two features of this shrine puzzled Kathleen Kenyon. Though it gave open evidence of dating back to the Neolithic, or new Stone Age period, it had not been suspected until now that Jericho had so venerable a past. Nor did archaelogists have previous proof that in this simple early farming era of man's development, there was formal worship or structures showing such sophistication in workmanship and imagery. Though this rich find could not be gone into and checked against other evidence and scientific examination of stratification and charcoal, by a method known as Carbon 14 (which came much later in her explorations), Kathleen Kenyon was already beginning to perceive that Jericho was a town built on towns, a culture built on cultures.

The 1953 season began with an investigation into tombs which was to continue, in relation with other explorations, for four more seasons. Kathleen Kenyon and her co-workers started with the Middle and Early Bronze Age tombs. The best large group of these was found on a bluff on the west side of a ravine, but it was slow, grueling work to remove the heavy granite stones which guarded them.

The small door blocking one of six look-alike tombs, was finally taken away. Kathleen Kenyon, wilted with fatigue, but terribly excited, crouched down on hands and knees and peered in. She could see nothing until her eyes grew accustomed to the gloom of the deep shaft. Even so, she could barely make out a chamber, somewhat rectangular, with very low roof. Then, straining her eyes even more, she caught sight of bodies laid away at least 3500 years before. Not until the next day, with a generator puffing away on the surface, and three lights suspended from it and focused inside the tomb (while an Arab foreman entangled himself in a cord and received a shock), could she make out the details.

She had thought the day before the bodies were laid out in a row, as if of equal importance. Now, on clearer inspection, she saw that the center of the tomb was occupied by a low platform of mud-brick. On it lay the remains of a man richly clad, his head raised on a stone pillow. He was obviously a man of some distinction. A number of earlier burials had been swept aside to give him more room, but there were four other burials of the same period: a woman, a young boy, and two children, set around the edge of the chamber.

Could the wife and children have been killed to accompany their master into the afterworld? If so, drinks had been provided for them, for there was a fine goblet. In addition, placed above the heads of all were large storage jars, a small dipper flask in the mouth of each jar, so that they could help themselves when thirsty. There was food, too, judging from the baskets and plates on the magnificent table, where bones of sheep reposed.

There were portions of two dismantled stools which must have been pushed through the small opening in the chamber. Obviously, Kathleen thought, the undertakers hadn't bothered to put them together again. She noted the molded legs swelling out into a curve, showing the Egyptian influence. It was easy to deduce from the workmanship that in this era, chisels, drills, even ripping saws and lathes, had been used. There were boxes of toilet articles in wicker baskets, and scattered about were beads, scarabs, and wooden combs lying near the skulls. There was even a henna-dyed wig.

The other five tombs, however, showed no evidence of any distinction in placement. All the bodies were laid out in rows.

Now that the tombs were opened, it was important to preserve their contents as soon as possible. Although four-thirty was the usual end of a working day that began very early, there were no limits now as to hours. Paraffin had to be dripped on the objects from a little saucepan heated on an Arab primus stove. Kathleen Kenyon, her photographer, technical expert, and three others sometimes stayed on until one o'clock in the morning.

Only one person at a time could crawl inside a tomb, so, crouched or lying in the entrance, Kathleen Kenyon cleaned each object within reach. Then, in bare feet, she stepped gingerly in. She bent double, and remained in that stiff position, for there was danger of damaging the delicate objects. None of them could be moved without first being coated with paraffin. As she worked inside the tomb, she could actually see wooden articles further inside cracking before her eyes because of exposure to air. Still, she could not hurry, for each object had to be handled with skill and care.

By careful examination of tombs and other findings, such as broken pot shards, Kathleen Kenyon traced Jericho through the fourth to sixth centuries A.D. Then, going farther, she traced it through the Iron Age, the later Bronze Age, and Middle and Early parts of the Bronze Age. She found a well-developed town life in the third millennium B.C. with strong defenses, bringing out how important Jericho was as a guardian gateway into Palestine from the east. Then, around 2000 B.C. came invasion. For a time the city appeared to have been occupied by nomadic people; between 1800-1600 B.C., there was once more a flourishing city with stronger walls than ever. Before she was through with her explorations in these later periods of Jericho, she found evidence of seventeen rebuilds of the so-called "Joshua" wall alone. Before she was through with all of her explorations, she found twenty-nine walls at Jericho!

Throughout her seasons at Jericho, she continued her tomb excavations into various periods, along with her other explorations. She found earlier tombs suggesting tribal groups with different customs. She found undisturbed multiple burials and tombs where the last occupants were carelessly tossed aside for newcomers. She found tombs containing food and drink, but only one containing weapons of defense. She found in the tombs pottery, bronze pins, scarabs, beads, portions of wooden furniture, wooden bowls, and in one a brain shriveled up inside a skull. She found an ancient tomb of great size, cut into rock, harboring a single person. When she examined his skeleton, his spine revealed he suffered from advanced osteoarthritis, just as does modern man.

In 1953, just as in her first season at Jericho when she came across the mysterious shrine, Kathleen Kenyon was drawn back again, as if by a magnet, to a much earlier period in Jericho's history.

As she was tracing a lower-level Jericho wall, she came upon a small group of superimposed houses. These houses astonished her. They had well-proportioned rectangular rooms, with solid walls of cigar-shaped brick bearing the thumb imprints of the brickmakers. They were of the same good architecture, and had the same polished floors of gypsum plaster and walls as did the ancient shrine which had intrigued her the year before. Beneath the floor of one house she found the remains of at least thirty persons, some buried in crouched position and intact; some with skulls, and even jaws, removed. Lying in discarded heaps beneath other excavations, Kathleen Kenyon found skillfully preserved plaster skull heads, one with a moustache added in paint.

The artistic know-how shown in the replicas of these ancient human faces, as well as in figurines and architecture, seemed incredible for so long ago. Surely this development showed indications of the city's belonging to a pre-pottery Neolithic Age. Scattered in the ruins were sickle blades, flint instruments, grinding querns, and polished stones. But she would jump to no conclusions until she had made many scientific tests of the stratification and charcoal known as Carbon 14. Even now, however, she was thrilled by her findings. She was certainly coming upon something of vital significance in Jericho's past.

By 1954 and 1955, newspapers, magazines and archaeological circles were vitally interested in the findings of Kathleen Kenyon at Jericho. The more she dug into the past, the farther back that past seemed to stretch.

No story since the discovery of King Tut's tomb in the Valley of Kings at Thebes, Egypt, back in the twenties, so aroused the public imagination, particularly in England

and Canada. For although the ancient Pharaoh's solid gold coffin and the rich records of an age, dating back thirty centuries, found in his tomb were more glittering than the tomb-findings at Jericho, Kathleen Kenyon was doing far more than exploring one tomb or one era. She was digging out the entire past of Jericho—a past of unbelievable antiquity.

Having traced Jericho from the fourth century A.D. back to the fourteenth century B.C., she was now discovering it had a much earlier beginning.

There was great excitement when she found that the brick rectangular houses she had come on earlier were not just a small group. Instead, they covered the entire eight-acre mound at Jericho, and they belonged to the pre-pottery Stone Age of history.

Already, through matching one type of pottery found at Jericho with that found on sites such as Yarmuk and Ros Sharsba, she knew now that Jericho was older than the oldest of these. And the "oldest" was a small primitive settlement which dated back to the second half of the fifth millennium! But at Jericho, she had found a second type of pottery, older than the first, and unique to this site.

To place Jericho still farther back, she had found a pre-pottery Neolithic town which was not, from indications, small and primitive, but large and surprisingly sophisticated for the early farming stage of man. It gradually became clear that Jericho's first citizens easily lived before all other Neolithic (or new Stone Age) peoples—that is, those who recently came from a hunting and cave-dwelling existence.

"Just how old was Jericho and what would Kathleen Kenyon find next?" people asked.

What Kathleen Kenyon found next, as she traced the settlement of pre-pottery Jericho, was a town wall. She found it beneath a deep tilled fill, sloping down over the face of another wall. This was very much older and more deeply sunk. The wall was set on bedrock below the surface of the first. It was connected with a great tower. When she made this fascinating discovery, the 1954 season was over, and it was not until 1955 that she could even begin to explore it.

The tower appeared far more impressive than she had expected to find at even a much later period. It stood out as a distinguished monument to the energy and skill of its Stone Age constructors. In the center was a small area, outlined by huge stone slabs.

Impatiently, Kathleen Kenyon waited, as soft soil was cleared away, and a flight of wide steps revealed itself. The steps led down into the very heart of the tower. As she started down the steps, formed of great slabs of stone, she glanced up toward the oblique roof built of even larger slabs. All were hammer-dressed to a fine finish.

She could not get over the splendor of this stairway. It reminded her of the great shafts found in Palestinian towns of a much later period. The walls, slightly concave, were covered with mud plaster. These, as did the hog-back rectangular houses, showed the fingermarks of their makers. These marks made the dim past seem very near and intimate.

She counted steps before she reached the bottom, then entered into a horizontal passage leading east, toward the center of town. Suddenly, her passage was blocked by fine earth, piled nearly to the ceiling. In the upper two feet of the ceilings were skeletons. She had often seen this arrangment in pre-pottery Jericho. There were eleven bodies, jammed in so tightly it would be difficult to disentangle them.

Kathleen Kenyon wondered if they were the last vain defenders of this town. She looked again and saw that the level in the passage had risen almost to where the bodies were piled. The tower must have gone out of effective use before the bodies were placed there.

She could only guess at the purpose of the stair and passage. She traced it some feet farther. It should have emerged from the wall of the tower, but it didn't, for the edge of the tower lay just beyond the excavation area.

By 1956, the greater part of the tower was cleared, but the base had not yet been reached.

When suntanned Kathleen Kenyon returned to London that summer to give lectures at the university and raise funds for her final season at Jericho, there was still mystery as to the purpose of the tower. She never did discover all its secrets. She did know, however, that the tower was a wonderful engineering feat. Though it had been built thousands of years before the Egyptian pyramids, she told reporters and an eager public, it still stood firm and impressive, in spite of the frequent earthquakes that shook the Jordan Valley.

This tower was at the rear of a mammoth wall, founded on rock. At the base of the wall was an irrigation ditch which encircled the settlement, and showed, as did the storage bins for water and other evidence found in town walls and structures, that pre-pottery Stone Age Jericho was far in advance of even much later times in bringing water artificially to its community. The ditch must have been a tremendous undertaking. Since they had no heavy picks, the workers must have broken and crushed the rock of which it was constructed using stone mauls of the sort found in great numbers on this site.

The season's excavations revealed that a layer of soft silt went over the top of the tower, and that the debris levels showed a complete break in Jericho's history. They indicated that two separate people lived at Jericho during the pre-pottery Stone Age period! One lived in long successions of superimposed houses Kathleen Kenyon had found during her first exploring seasons at Jericho. There were twenty successive phases of these houses. The houses were very well built, and there were many evidences of a developed communal life undreamed of for this early farming period in man's history. "It was like finding something the size of New York City in Caesar's time," she said.

Some of these houses had now been traced back to the second half of the seventh millennium B.C. They preceded by over two thousand years the earliest primitive villages found so far on other Near East sites. The story of this pre-pottery town showed an almost modern, or at least Medieval, stage of development except for lacking written records which did not appear until the third millennium B.C. There was evidence that the "plaster-floor" group had lived at Jericho for a considerable time, and some of their houses, when examined, might prove older than those already studied, she admitted.

Moreover, there was an earlier period in Jericho's history still. For now, in several areas, appeared an entirely different type of house. The walls of these houses were curved and the rooms almost round. The roofs gave evidence of having been domed and built of bricks of a flat base. The floors and walls were cruder than in the other houses. They were covered with an unburnished mud plaster. The rooms were sunken with entrance passages sloping down into them, and in one house Kathleen Kenyon found steps with wooden treads.

Undoubtedly, the people who occupied the round houses lived at Jericho before the others. The rectangular-house people must have overthrown them.

How old was Jericho? At the end of the 1957 season, Kathleen Kenyon had examined these earlier houses, and traced some of them back to 7800 B.C., but Jericho might be even older than that, she conceded. How old was Jericho? Who could really say? One thing was certain. Kathleen Kenyon, who had begun with a "limited" digging-out of the Joshua era, had gone on from there to uncover not only the lowest town in the world, but the oldest known town in the world!

»»

Kathleen Kenyon, however, did not rest on the laurels of her brilliant explorations at Jericho. After receiving honors at Oxford and her alma mater, Somerville College, she wrote and lectured in England and America. Then she went back to her diggings. As director of the British School of Archaeology in Jerusalem, she returned to the Near East. By 1962, she was hard at work on a series of excavations around the old city of Jerusalem, exposing remains of a Canaanite wall, as early as c.1800 B.C.

In spite of her devotion to archaeology, she finds time for recreation, both between and during her exploration seasons. She likes horseback riding and plays a good game of lawn tennis. Her interest in young people, which made her take time off from her absorbing life work during World War II to direct the Youth Department of the British Red Cross, still remains. She has trained many students in archaeology.

Kathleen Kenyon has come a long way since she was born on January 5, 1906, in an English manor house. She has covered an enormous number of miles in her diggings, both at home and abroad. Undoubtedly, she will win new honors for her valuable contributions to the world's knowledge. Most likely, however, she will best be remembered for her digging far down into Jericho's thrilling and almost continuous past, and coming up with the oldest town in the world.

LOUISE ARNER BOYD

There are certain regions of the world which stubbornly resist man's efforts to explore. Even today, there are cruel deserts, towering mountains, steaming jungles, and vast frozen wastes which have baffled explorers from earliest times.

Such a region is the Arctic around Spitsbergen, Franz Josef Land, and Greenland. Although this group of polar islands was, even before the days of the Norsemen, among the first terrains to be visited, and later became a challenge to explorers from many nations seeking a northwest passage to China and India, the topography of this bleak area remained a mystery for centuries.

Early maps, charts, and sketches were largely figments of

the imagination of cartographers remaining safely at home. These makers of maps depended on the tales of returning travelers with only the scantiest knowledge of geography, and no scientific means for evaluating the chameleon-like, jagged shorelines.

The need for accurate knowledge—maps and photographs of this fiord-indented polar region—became of vital concern to America when our country found itself more and more enmeshed in World War II. Before America's actual entrance into the war, Germany was in possession of Scandinavian countries which controlled this strategic part of North America. It became imperative for the United States to have up-to-date data on these islands. The ice-packed coastlines with many hidden harbors would prove excellent lurking places for German U-boats, ready to strike out at Allied shipping in this hemisphere.

An explorer, an American woman named Louise Arner Boyd, had for many years been engaged in making expeditions to this little-known Arctic country. Eight times she had gone to Spitsbergen, Franz Josef Land, and Greenland on fact-finding, peaceful explorations, beginning in August, 1924. By the end of 1938 she had gathered a wealth of material. These were carefully researched maps, written records, and excellent photographs of fiords, glaciers, ice-topped mountains, as well as data on the people, animal life, geology, and physiography.

Now, in the fall of 1940, her well-advanced plans to publish her findings under the auspices of the American Geographical Society were brought to a halt. Because of the importance of her explorations, the United States government requested she defer publication of her book and make her intimate knowledge available only to government officials. Louise Arner Boyd did not hesitate. Not only did she immediately "put into security" all material painstakingly collected, but included her extensive library of photographs taken on all her explorations.

In June, 1941, she was chosen to head the investigation of magnetic and radio phenomena in Greenland and other Arctic regions. She also worked in cooperation with the National Bureau of Standards, and acted as technical expert for the War Department, but it was not until some years after the close of World War II that Louise Arner Boyd's life as an Arctic explorer and her part in America's war effort became known to the public.

San Rafael, California, where Louise Arner Boyd was born September 16, 1887, would seem a world apart from Spitsbergen, Franz Josef Land, and Greenland, under the glittering ice-eye of the North Pole. Yet throughout her childhood and schooldays at Miss Stewart's School in San Rafael and at Miss Murison's School in San Francisco, Louise found it easy to dream of travel, especially of travel to faraway places.

There was no more inspiring place for a wide-eyed, adventurous girl or boy to grow up than around San Francisco, that throbbing seafaring city where American pioneer spirit and Oriental flavor mingled. As she rode on the ferries plying between San Francisco and her home on the outskirts, the deep-throated foghorns from great ships coming and going in the bay became familiar sounds to her. And sometimes she saw seamen with tipsy gait walking San Francisco's hilly, salt-sprayed streets as if still clinging to storm-tossed decks. They brought reminders of distant places—China, Japan, and the Philippines, as well as places to the Far North.

For just as a Gold Rush had brought many families, including hers, to the Far West, now another Gold Rush to the north was on. Thousands were answering the new siren call. Louise was three years old in 1890 when the big push toward Alaska and the Yukon began. It was to continue until she was a young lady.

Louise's father, John Franklin, was a wealthy mining operator. The family was well satisfied with California and comfortably rooted in their beautiful home, Maple Lawn, but others were pulling up stakes and heading north. From playmates, schoolmates, and grown-ups, Louise heard lurid accounts of northern adventures.

There were stories of fortunes made and lost up north; of sailors drugged and shanghaied, then thrown on board leaky north-bound boats; of panhandlers in Alaska wandering away from companions, to disappear forever in the unfamiliar frozen wastelands.

At home and at school, maps and globes of the world were eagerly examined. But most of the places mentioned were not recorded.

Even less explicit, she soon discovered, were the maps of another Arctic region now being widely talked about. Up in an icy region called Greenland, far to the northeast of Alaska, connected by the Arctic Ocean, Admiral Robert Peary was searching for the North Pole.

Louise was only four years old when Peary proved that Greenland was an island. But she was eleven when he formed the Peary Arctic Club and published *Northwest Over the Great Ice* in 1898.

She read books about the Arctic, including Peary's and his wife's diary, fascinated. But the descriptions and maps of this region of ice-floes seemed unsatisfying and contradictory. "If only I could go up to the Arctic and see for myself," she thought.

But many years would pass before Louise's dream of Arctic explorations could be realized. Long before that time, Admiral Peary would have reached the North Pole in 1909. And for years, a Captain Cook would challenge his claim, saying he had arrived there first. Peary would finally be acknowledged as the rightful discoverer.

By then, Louise would be a woman in her thirties. For all

her gentle feminine charm and lovely blue eyes, she would be a purposeful woman, a cosmopolitan woman. She would have many interests and hobbies, including gardening and horseback riding, and, surprising to some, shooting. Later, she would be credited with shooting twenty-nine polar bears during her Arctic exploratons.

From earliest years, Louise had a good business head, too, and, after her father's death in 1920, became President of the Boyd Investment Company in San Francisco. She had money and time enough to finance her own expeditions, and plan her own itineraries.

She had studied not only geography, but botany, geology, topography, and photography. She had traveled to northern countries of Europe, including old Poland, with her brothers Seth and John, Jr., and returned home to compile a book, illustrated with good maps of the varied countrysides and heartwarming photographs of the people. She would be ready at last for her much more difficult adventure.

In August, 1924, Louise Arner Boyd stood on the deck of a small Norwegian tourist steamer, camera in hand. She had told her friends back in San Francisco that she was merely going on a summer cruise when she set out, but she knew in her heart that this journey to the Arctic was in the nature of a probing tour. It was a serious project which would absorb her life more and more.

She watched the pack-ice swirl dangerously down the forbidden coastline. Then, as they approached Spitsbergen, a heavy fog descended. Later she was to grow accustomed to sudden heavy fogs and snowstorms, even in midsummer. Now the steamer cruised offshore blindly; the captain hoping the fog would lift so that they could make shore. This was the only season of the year when ice-floes did not seal off the coastline. The fog persisted, and Louise put aside her camera for the time being. The mountains and glaciers of Spitsbergen were now invisible.

Recalling the history of this land of Arctic islands she had read about as a girl, Louise felt a sudden bond with explorers of the past—Svalbard, the Icelandic seafarer who came here in 1194. He, as well as Jacob van Heemskerk and Cornelis-zoon Rijp, two Dutchmen who visited this mountainous, snow-covered polar region in 1596, had been stopped by the same fog which now frustrated her plans to go ashore and take pictures.

Nevertheless, that summer, and for years to come, Louise Arner Boyd would see and examine much Arctic terrain. Traveling by steamer, motor dory and Eskimo dog sled, this vital American woman, rosy-cheeked and friendly, would turn up before dawn in many a lonely Arctic cabin in this sparsely settled country which had only occasional settlements of Norwegian and Danish miners, trappers, and wireless operators. She would learn more about the polar region from these rugged wayfarers than from any other sources.

She made a small beginning that first summer. Spitsbergen, she soon discovered, was an island area of more than 23,000 square miles, more than half of which was covered by ice even in summer. Along the west coast she found mountains with sharp ridges and peaks and, in the southern part of Vestspitsbergen, the highest mountain of all.

She took advantage of every chance she could to carry her camera to high ground, as she did on all later explorations. In that way, she could get wide and distant views. There was really no other way to gain a clear idea of the topography of this frozen country.

The many large fiords which pierced the west and north coasts of Vestspitsbergen fascinated her. So did the Dutch-sounding names such as Hornsund, Bellsund, Van Mijenfjorden, and Van Keulenfjorden. She eagerly examined the east coast formed by a front of inland ice. Many of the glaciers reached the sea, but in Vestspitsbergen she found massive ice-free valleys and coastal plains formed by the sea when its level was much higher than now.

Although Louise Boyd did not regard herself as an expert botanist, she studied with interest the carpets of bright green moss with golden flowers on the higher slopes above the sea. Occasionally, she was thrilled by the sight of a bright poppy. She collected samples of flowers and fauna for her California friend Alice Eastman, an internationally known botanist, to analyze and catalogue. She studied the trees of the region, too, amused by their puniness when compared with California's giant redwoods. She found here only the polar willow, not more than two inches tall, and, more rarely, the dwarf birch.

In the years to come, Louise Arner Boyd would explore every fiord and passageway to which ice conditions permitted entry in many an Arctic locale. Either by ship or small boat, she would study them from King Oscar Fiord north to Cape Montpensier at the northeast corner of Île de France. She would make frequent landings for firsthand investigations of features which interested her particularly. She would make detailed studies, maps, and photographic records. She would collect botanical specimens wherever she went. Sometimes her base of operations would be the ship chartered and financed by herself. Sometimes she would work out from camp sites—her tent pitched in frozen wastes under the great Arctic moons.

Louise would come back again and again and, whenever she came, she would make new friends with the people, and find more to interest her, for she had fallen in love with the Arctic long before she ever saw it.

In the summer of 1926, Louise Arner Boyd returned to the Far North, chartering a Norwegian sealer, the *Hobby*, and made a detailed tour of Franz Josef Land, lying east of Spitsbergen and north of Novaya Zemlya. The ice-capped islands she visited had a monotonous appearance at first, but soon her growingly expert eye caught points of differences. The topography and scanty vegetation made Franz Josef Land resemble Spitsbergen somewhat, though she found many more species of birds here than elsewhere. Aside from the native Eskimos, she met only occasional wireless operators and trappers.

Since she was now resolved to return to this part of the world often, and investigate every feature of its wild, primitive life, she began on her second trip to build up a photographic record of Arctic topography of sea and ice. This became her special field on all future expeditions. She also began to assemble a competent staff of co-workers.

When, in the summer of 1928, Louise Boyd once more chartered the *Hobby* and sailed forth on further Arctic explorations, she ran into unexpected adventure.

Late in May, 1928, when General Nobilie's airship, *Italia* —returning from the North Pole—was wrecked, Roald Amundsen, the daring Norwegian explorer who had twice circled the North Pole in 1926 in the dirigible, the *Norge*, was again exploring the polar region.

Amundsen volunteered to go in search of him, and left Bergen for Spitsbergen in an airplane on June 17. By the time Louise and her party arrived there, he had been missing for weeks. Now, abandoning her own working schedule, Louise and her expedition started in search of Amundsen. It was a long, costly search, for they traveled over ten thousand miles to many points along the west coast of Spitsbergen, then east to Franz Josef Land. From there, they went north into pack-ice to latitude 81 degrees, 13', then westward into the Greenland Sea.

In spite of their most diligent efforts, however, Amundsen was never found nor heard of again, but Louise Arner Boyd never regretted having put aside her own plans to aid in searching for him.

By the year 1931, Louise had found a Norwegian sailing vessel, *Veslekari*, which pleased her so well that it was to become her "home away from home" on all future explorations to the Far North. For many years thereafter, this stalwart ship was a familiar sight at Alesund, Norway, where it was outfitted for each new Boyd expedition.

In it she made her first explorations of Greenland, that fascinating land where Eric the Red came at the end of the tenth century, and Henry Hudson on a voyage undertaken in 1607. On the northwestern coast at Inglefield gulf, Robert Peary had spent the winter of 1893 with a party of thirteen, including his wife. His daughter, the first American child to be born in the Arctic, was born there.

East Greenland now became the focal point of Louise Arner Boyd's explorations. Her first trip was largely a photographic expedition. Her object was to examine and photograph every inlet and sound in the area of Franz Josef and King Oscar Fiords. She also began a more extensive botanical collection for her friend Alice Eastman to analyze and catalogue later.

Louise looked upon the 1931 expedition to East Greenland as a reconnaissance. On the basis of it, she planned future expeditions. There was no day long enough for her now. She determined to investigate this region until she had seen not only those parts accessible by ship and record them with camera as faithfully as she could, but also to explore the inaccessible.

Brief though these summer months were when her ship could pass through the coastal ice belt and come out again,

This map is based on one prepared by Louise Boyd for the American Geographical Society. It shows East Greenland which Louise Boyd visited several times in the 1930's.

she accomplished miracles her first season in Greenland. She came away with several thousand excellent photographs, including a series which covered a newly-found connection between Kjerulf and Didson Fiords. She made, too, what is believed to be the first penetration by ship into Ice Fiord, discovering the De Geer Glacier which entered the head of the fiord from the north. It did not occur to the modest Louise Arner Boyd to plant a flag and stake a claim to her discoveries.

One of her most interesting experiences that summer was a visit to the Eskimo settlement of Scoresbysund. This remote settlement, which with two other small ones made up the northernmost colony on the east coast of Greenland, was seldom visited by outsiders. One peaceful August evening, the sailing ship *Veslekari* anchored in Rosenvinge Bay, just off the main settlement. The Danes and Eskimos hurried out to meet them, as did two aviators who had lately landed from Europe. Some came in launches; some in kayaks. As the kayaks paddled swiftly toward Louise and her group, the round-faced, grinning Eskimos put on a "command" performance for their benefit. To demonstrate their skill and fearlessness, they turned their kayaks over and over in the water.

As the Boyd expedition was escorted to shore, the Eskimos pulled their kayaks from the water and set them upside down on racks to dry. Louise and her party passed other wooden racks where seal meat, the main Eskimo food, was drying. The meat hung in strips, high enough from the ground to be out of reach of the numerous yapping dogs and wild bears.

The town was built on the southern slope of a hill, Louise now noticed. There was the house of the administrator of the colony and his family—spic and prim. There was a church with an adjoining rectory; a store; worksheds; a house occupied by the wireless operator and his wife and big enough for guests. There were also the homes of the Danish townspeople, and the lesser dwellings of the Eskimos.

As the Danes asked Louise Boyd many questions about the outside world and her work, the Eskimo men danced, chanted, and sang for them—their knee-high sealskin boots and colorful costumes contrasting with the plain tin pans they beat on, as substitutes for drums.

In the fading light, the Lutheran church—a wooden structure painted dark red with white window sills—seemed quaintly old-worldish. Over the entrance was a great clock, and above it, a glittering bronze bell. Inside, the church was finished in natural wood. It was a simple dignified meeting-house, from the ceiling of which hung a ship model, *William Scoresby, Jr.* It was a replica, Louise learned, of one in Denmark. There were three circular chandeliers; a clean white linen altar cloth on the altar, with a cross and two candlesticks above the altar.

On Sunday, eleven in Louise's group, the two aviators, Danish townsfolk, and twenty-seven Eskimos attended divine service. With the first tolling of the bell, the congregation went to the side of the building and stood there facing the sound. At the second tolling, they all marched to the front of the building, but remained outside. Only at the third tolling of the bell did they enter. Then, with few exceptions, the men sat on the left, the women on the right, as in early Puritan meeting-houses in America. Except for a short talk in Danish, and a prayer for the visitors to have safe voyages home, the service was conducted in Greenlandic. When it was over, the Boyd expedition accompanied the genial pastor and his wife to the manse, and enjoyed their hospitality over coffee. It was a brief respite from the ordeals of the Arctic wastes—a bit of civilization in the midst of frozen silent wilderness.

Later that day, they took some of the Eskimos back to

their homes at Cape Hope and Cape Steward. En route, a bitter wind blew eastward off an inland ice cap. Suddenly, the decks of the *Veslekari* were cleared of Eskimos, who scurried off to the engine room to keep warm. Louise had to laugh at these "tenderfoots."

It was past three in the morning when the Eskimos reappeared, and left the ship. The women and children went ashore in launches, the men in kayaks, racing each other to land. Against the early rays of dawn, their black silhouettes made a long-to-be-remembered picture in her mind. As they reached shore, she saw seven brilliant flashes of light, followed by seven stacatto-like rifle shots. The captain of the *Veslekari* acknowledged the Eskimos' salute by tooting the boat's whistle. Then the Eskimos repeated their salute, and, as they lined up on shore, waved good-by.

By the summer of 1933, Louise Boyd had assembled her permanent crew. From then on, Captain Johan Olsen, his first officer, Captain Peter Eliassen, and the engineer, Peter Strand, were to be familiar faces on her future expeditions to East Greenland. So were some members of her scientific staff, and the brave men she met summer after summer at the Danish and Norwegian wireless stations, as well as hunters in many an isolated cabin.

Much of her success in her Arctic explorations she owed to her ability for bringing together the right people. The teamwork of her group was excellent. This and the aid of Arctic natives, who freely gave of their time and first-hand knowledge of unfamiliar country, helped to make each succeeding expedition more satisfying. Throughout her summers there, the American Geographical Society gave her much helpful advice on how best to plan her time and resources.

On all but the first of her East Greenland explorations, tide gauges loaned by the United States Coast and Geodetic

Survey were carried on her ship. On later explorations, important tide records of some length were made at various sea and land locations.

Her ship was also equipped with an echo sounder, and because of the value of the sounding work done on her 1933 expedition, she engaged a hydrographer for the next two expeditions.

While making the first run to test their sound recorder off the northwest coast of the Lofoten and Vesteraalen Islands, the instrument suddenly recorded shallow depths, not usually produced by soft or hard bottom. Captain Olsen was deeply puzzled. Suspecting that what was being recorded were massed bodies of the great schools of fish known to be in these waters during summer, he ordered the ship turned about. His surmise was right. Henceforth, manufacturers called this type of echo sounder the *Veslekari* model. Afterwards, it was used by trawlers off the Norwegian coast for locating cod and herring.

The expedition now included a surveyor, assistant surveyor, a physiographer, a geologist, and Louise as the leader and official photographer. Although she had now included a professional botanist, he developed appendicitis and had to be sent home on a Norwegian whaler, so Louise once more became the expedition's only botanist.

She did much better than she expected, too—collecting eight vascular plants at thirteen locations that season, besides carrying on a full program as official photographer. By the time the summer was ended, she had added several thousand photographs of land and sea ice, glacial marginal features, land forms, and vegetation, to her growing East Greenland collection.

She and her staff had also introduced new methods of surveying in the field, and had made three large-scale, detailed maps of glaciers, as well as a map of the never-before-explored Gregory Valley at the head of Franz Josef Fiord. The maps were later published in color, with a full report of the expedition.

Louise Boyd planned the 1937 and 1938 expeditions as a unit. In general, she hoped to carry on the scientific program begun in 1933. If weather conditions permitted, she and her team would work their way progressively northward along the coast. They would focus on the King Oscar-Franz Josef Fiord region. For there was much in this region that was still an enigma. As matters turned out, it was 1938 before they could penetrate these unexplored areas.

The scientific staff now included Louise Boyd, leader and photographer; Dr. Richard Foster Flint, geologist; Dr. A. Lincoln Washburn, assistant geologist; Dr. Henry J. Oosting, botanist; F. W. Buhler, surveyor; James M. Le Roy, hydrographer; Sverre S. Semoy, radio operator. Again she engaged the same captain and engineer, and several of the 1933 crew.

As usual, the outfitting of the *Veslekari* was done at Alesund, Norway. By June 1, they were ready to sail for Troms, and pick up other staff members. They were delayed, however, by failure of the sonic depth finger they had rented from a London firm, the same instrument they had rented in 1933. Finally, they agreed to buy a new instrument, but the fastest service meant sending the instrument by way of Sweden; then by rail to Narvik. Rather than wait at Alesund, Norway, however, they sailed away on June 4, spending nearly two weeks on their journey north. They had plenty to occupy them, however, for they found many points of interest along the coast, and stopped off at offshore islands, at inviting spots in the Lofoten and Vesteraalen Islands; at Rost and Veroy Islands with their rookeries, the nesting place of thousands of exotic Arctic birds.

They were anxious, nonetheless, to be on their way, and delighted when the new sounder arrived at Narvik on June 16. On June 18, it was installed, and the engineer who brought it aboard set out for a trial run. Louise stood by him eagerly as they put out to open sea off Andeenes Light.

On June 22, to their great surprise, the sounder readings rose sharply from normal sea floor depths to some 320 fathoms. This emphasized the importance of keeping the sounder operating whenever possible on a journey such as theirs for it soon became clear they had come upon a previously unrecorded ocean bank. Verifying this by further soundings, they returned to the mainland. They reached Troms June 25, and there the sounder expert left them on their own. They were not at all worried. The sounder, having met all tests satisfactorily, was readily accepted; from then on, it became an important feature of Louise Boyd's Arctic equipment.

It was a happy, well-trained group—all cheerful, intelligent, indispensable—who were with Louise on this expedition. On June 30, with complete staff, they sailed away from Troms, heading north for Bear Island. They spent July 2 on the island, stopping first on the south side, then going farther east to the wireless station. At three-thirty in the morning, the Boyd party routed the sleepy station personnel from their beds. As had happened so many times before, they were given a hearty welcome. Coffee was brewed, and as they sat drinking it, warming themselves by the fire, endless questions were asked and answered.

Next day, the *Veslekari* set course for Jan Mayen Island. No sooner did they start out than a strong southeast gale lashed them. Heavy seas soon swept over the decks, putting so much water on them that the iron door of the galley had to be closed to keep water from splashing on the stove and broiling the cook. Everyone dashed for hip rubbers—an absolute necessity now. In spite of these aids, the sea surged around their legs in the mess room, often reaching knee-depth. To add to their woes, the sounder refused to work, and most of the time the ship had to be navigated at from half to slow speed.

In spite of bad weather and the many complications, however, the Boyd party would not be cheated out of their Fourth of July. Just as if she were back home, Louise and the others ran Old Glory up to the masthead and celebrated Independence Day in true American style!

By July 6, the storm was just about over. It was a great relief to run into calm sea again, with long easy roll, but low fog now made for poor visibility. It was not until their echo sounder recorded shallowing depths that they were even aware of approaching land. Soon they heard crashing breakers on the beach, then, through the fog, they glimpsed the comforting land. They were just off Jan Mayen Island, but not until shortly before noon the next day did the heavy fog lift so that they could make shore. They entered Jameson Bay, and dropped anchor off a Norwegian wireless and meteorological station.

Once again they made friends, and took a breather from their explorations. They remained at the station until July 11, going out on short expeditions to study the South Glacier. Here, too, they did the first map work of this expedition.

Louise spent much of her time with her camera on the glacier, and taking long hikes over the volcanic terrain of the island with its "spatter cones" and extinct craters. This was a most exhilarating experience for her. When weather was good, Mount Beerenberg loomed up in majestic glory, eight thousand feet, "a glacier-hung summit, a weather breeder and catcher of clouds and fog, gleaming in the sunlight," Louise Boyd later described it.

If, on her return to business affairs in San Francisco, Louise walked with taller gait, it must be remembered she had visited those magic lands of ice, and reached a grandeur of height and view which only a handful of explorers had reached before.

She had gone to the Arctic for love of the region and to search out its mysteries. She had not gone there for honors. Yet, as the years passed, honors came to her.

In 1939, she received honorary degrees from the University of California and from Mills College. The American Geographical Society gave her a gold medal, and her home town, San Rafael, gave her a parade, and made her an honorary citizen for her brave achievements as a woman explorer. When World War II was finally over, the United States Army gave her a certificate of appreciation for the part she played in helping to win it.

Abroad, too, Louise was soon recognized for her Arctic achievements. France gave her the Chevalier Legion of Honor decoration; Norway made her the first foreign woman to receive their St. Olaf of Norway award; she was given the Andree plaque by the Swedish Anthropological and Geographical Society. Denmark awarded her the medal of King Christian X.

The Society of Woman Geographers, of which she is a long-time member, consider her one of their most valuable members.

In 1955, Louise Arner Boyd, at the age of sixty-eight, took one more trip to the Arctic, flying over the North Pole in a private chartered plane and reviving many rich memories of this glacial land. But no one, not the Norsemen, not Peary, Amundsen, or herself, had really conquered its inscrutable, fiord-indented shores. Although Louise had photographed and mapped its little-known regions, it was still a land of wild deep mysteries. It still sealed off its shorelines for many months each year. It still sent out ice-floes to ensnare shipping far away. It still challenged men and women to come and tame it if they dared!

ISABELLA LUCY BIRD BISHOP

"I have only one formidable rival in Isabella's heart," Doctor John Bishop said facetiously, when he and Isabella Lucy Bird were married early in 1881, "and that is the high tablelands of Central Asia."

From her past record as a world traveler, the greying, bespectacled Edinburgh surgeon had reason to assume that his soft-spoken English bride, who stood only four feet, eleven inches in her high-button shoes, was still a rover at heart. Although she was almost fifty years old when they were wed at the small church St. Lawrence, Barton-on-the-Heath in Warwickshire, he was modest enough to believe that he had wooed and won her only because she had been "grounded" in

Edinburgh for four years. This, despite their mutual interests in botany, medicine, and books.

Indeed, had it not been for the invalidism of her beloved sister, Henrietta, in that Scotch city, he was certain Isabella would have been on her way long ago to places like Tibet, India, Persia, Korea, and China. Having been to many primitive parts of the globe, including Canada, Australia, the Sandwich Islands, the Rocky Mountains of America, little explored parts of Japan, as well as to China and Malacca, it was to the exotic tablelands of Central Asia that Isabella's large animated eyes turned most often when they scanned world maps together.

Now Henrietta was dead, and instead of taking instant "wing," as the doctor had feared she would, Isabella accepted his most recent proposal of marriage. Not only that, but she married him while still wearing mourning clothes. With true Victorian womanliness, she seemed content to settle down in dour Edinburgh, while he went on with his practice as surgeon at the Edinburgh Infirmary. Not even when Queen Victoria visited the hospital, and, at a reception, complimented Isabella on bringing glory to English womanhood by her daring explorations and books of travel and asked her what itinerary she planned next, did Isabella Bishop weaken.

"Oh, Your Majesty, I have settled down to domestic tranquility," she said with a sweet smile. "I have even taken to riding horseback sidesaddle, in deference to my growing elderliness."

At this the queen's eyes twinkled. "Ah, but you rode sidesaddle once before in your twenties," she reminded Isabella. "That was when you were carrying the mail bag in the Rocky Mountains of America. I remember the incident in one of your books well. You had ridden astraddle for hundreds of miles through wilderness, dressed in 'The American Lady's Mountain Dress.' I believe it was a half-fitting jacket with full

Turkish trousers gathered in frills at your ankles. On approaching Denver, you exchanged this bold attire for decorous long skirt. Then you rode sidesaddle into town so as not to offend the sensibilities of the 'natives.' Are you sure you are riding sidesaddle now in deference to your elderliness, rather than in deference to the 'natives'?"

As the gathering of Scotch and English celebrities smiled at the queen's wit, she leaned over and said softly to Isabella: "People like you and me never really settle down, Isabella. I expect to read more exciting chapters from your life one of these days."

Later, in her comfortable drawing room at 12 Walker Street, Edinburgh, surrounded by trophies of her colorful past, Isabella wondered if the queen was right. On other occasions, too, she had "settled down"—to nurse her ailing mother; to try a whirl at society which soon bored her. Always the call to ferret out distant lands compelled her again and again to set forth all alone, exchanging home hearthfires and familiar faces and customs for mountain campfires, volcanic eruptions, and strange peoples and ways.

"But I was single then," she reminded herself firmly. "Now I have found the dearest husband and companion in the world. Besides—I am too old and frail to rough it ever again . . ."

She had been young and frail when she started her adventurous life. Indeed, so frail was she when she was born on October 15, 1831, at Boroughbridge Hall in Yorkshire, that neighbors predicted so puny a child could never reach puberty. When her clergyman father moved to Tattenhall in Cheshire—she was three then—he carried her on a pillow on horseback. For years after, he continued to carry her on a pillow, as he made the rounds of his extensive parish on horseback, for he was determined to turn her into a hardy child and a horsewoman, or let her die in the attempt. He succeeded in turning her into a skilled horsewoman, at least, while her erudite mother taught her etiquette, languages, letters, and domestic skills. Though still frail when she entered her teens, she was a thoroughly rounded Victorian maiden, with a built-in resoluteness commonplace to many clergymen's children.

A spinal trouble, which bothered her from infancy, was still with her, even after an operation. When she was twenty-two, the family doctor advised a sea voyage. Her father pressed on her one hundred pounds, telling her she was free to travel until the money ran out. She went to Canada and America with relatives. She returned home seven months later, her health somewhat better, exciting stories to tell, and ten pounds in her pocket. Soon she was introduced to the publisher, John Murray, and her popular book, *The English Woman in America* appeared in 1856.

"You see," said her father, as her ten pounds grew into substantial money of her own, "the heavenly supply is always there, Isabella. We need only avail ourselves of the loaves and the fishes." It was a lesson in arithmetic Isabella never forgot.

For one thing, she could carry out a dream she had had for some time—to provide deep sea fishing boats for use of the poor people of West Highlands of Scotland, a section where the Bird family spent their summers.

Since her family had need for her domestic talents, she "settled down" to become a devoted Victorian daughter. Then her father died, and with a small inheritance, her mother, her sister Henrietta, and she moved to "The Cottage" in Edinburgh. But Isabella's gifts, humor, and charm were not born to blush unseen. In literary circles, she soon became a sensation. She could have basked in an easy social success and married the first likely suitor, but social life soon bored her, and she found herself running away to rough it among the islands of the Hebrides, where the welfare of the crofters became her personal concern.

After her mother's death, Isabella's health took a turn for the worse again, and once more she was urged by her doctor and sister Henrietta to try a sea voyage. In July, 1872, she sailed for Australia, spending three months there and in New Zealand. When she reached the Sandwich Islands (later the Hawaiian Islands) her inquisitive exploring nature really asserted itself. Her health much improved by her life in the out-of-doors, she spent several months in the archipelago, probing regions little known to the white residents. She went to live among the Polynesian natives. Here she made expeditions up and down the sharp ravines, first by mule, then on a spirited, unshod horse whose swimming prowess saved her life once, as she crossed a roaring, flooded river.

While on the island of Hawaii, she became intrigued with the volcano of Mauna Loa. It was active again, she was told, and a steamer was leaving for the vicinity. Determined to get it, she "galloped off," as she wrote her sister, "my saddle slipped over the horse's head. First my veil blew away, then my plaid, but in twenty minutes I had ridden down a descent of 2000 feet in time to board the '*Kilauea*.' Mr. W. then arrived with the carpet bag, then the Chinaman with a bag of oddments, next a native who had picked up the plaid and the specimens, ferns on the road, etc., so all was well."

Once arrived at her island destination, Isabella joined an English scientist, Mr. Green, to visit Mauna Loa. In spite of intense cold and the illness of a native guide, Isabella and the scientist ascended Mauna Loa successfully. "Cut, singed, grimy," she wrote, "with my thick gloves shrivelled off by the touch of sulphurous acid, and my boots utterly burned off. But what are cuts, bruises, fatigue and singed eyebrows in comparison with the awful sublimities I have witnessed today?"

Then Mr. Green left Isabella to her own devices, and she set out to visit the volcano of Kilauea alone. She penetrated a most desolate region, a region waterless, silent, hollow, and porous—"all cracks and fissures nefariously concealed by scrub and fern. I found a place, as I thought, free from risk, and was giving Kaheté, my horse, a feed of oats on my plaid, but before he finished them there was a rumbling and a vibration, and he went into the ground up above the knees, so snatching up the plaid, and jumping on him, I galloped away."

It took Isabella seven hours to get back to shelter and the welcome of the kindly Polynesian natives. She remained with them for some time, taking part in their daily lives, helping them to round up cattle, sharing in their sports, eating two-fingered poi with them on their mats, as if she had been doing such things all her life. Never had she felt more at home among any people. Never had she felt so peaceful and secure. She was sorry their numbers were dwindling fast, and that soon this fun-loving group might vanish. She knew this lotus-like existence was not for her permanently so, in 1873, she left the Sandwich Islands and sailed to America.

There she headed straight for the Rocky Mountains where she spent months in the highland valley of Estes Park, at a height of 7500 feet, not far from Longs Peak. Among the rough pioneer settlers and trappers of this solitary country, she was soon a great favorite, and a ranchman named Evans and his wife gave her shelter in their log ranch cabin.

Her life in the Rocky Mountains was in sharp contrast to that in the indolent Sandwich Islands. Here she found lonely, rugged, glorious country, inhabited mostly by mountain lions, grizzly bears, elk, mountain sheep, wolves, lynx, spotted deer, chipmunks, eagles, and rattlesnakes. There were also skunks, one of which made his lair under the Evanses' cabin until expelled.

She would gladly have paid her way for sharing in this

new life, but the Evanses, discovering her culinary talent, made her chief cook at six dollars a week. She remained on through the winter. She also took part in cattle roundups, and on one occasion hunted out the wild Texas cattle from snow-bound canyons, driving them down into lower pastures.

When the thaw came, she was on her way again, setting out all alone by horseback for Denver, Colorado. Avoiding towns as much as she could, she found friendly accommodation at night among the rude settlers in sections where there were no hotels or taverns. At one such ranchhouse, she was regaled with fearful tales of violence, vigilance committees, lynch law, and "stringings." When she remarked she had spent the preceding night at Hall's Gulch, two old women in the homespun parlor shook their heads in distress.

"Why, a man was strung up there only yesterday," said one. "Didn't you see him dangling from the big tree there? 'Twould be enough to curdle a body's blood to stay in that gulch alone at night. And you actually slept there, and saw nary a ghost?"

"Nary a ghost," said Isabella, grinning.

Soon the tiny English lady, who looked like a big-eyed, wondering child, but possessed the courage of a lion, became a favorite wherever she roamed. She was given sage and sometimes contradictory advice by old-timers as to the best trails to follow. Sometimes they insisted on giving her personal escort. She received proposals of marriage, too, from young men and old, but with great tact she declined, with the mental reservation that if she married at all, it would be to a "home" lad.

Finally she arrived at Denver, only to find a financial crisis there. The bank was unable to cash her circulatory notes, and her funds were alarmingly low. However, undaunted, she went on to beautiful Green Lake, 12,000 feet high, and thoroughly enjoyed the scenery. Then at Georgetown, she was invited to carry the mail bag on her way back to the Evanses' ranch. This she did, for a small token payment.

With this weighty load, she made "the long ascent to the gates of rock at a height of 9000 feet through the wildest and most wonderful scenery for twenty miles." She crossed thirteen ranges from 9000 to 11,000 feet high, passing through eery canyons and gulches, crossing thirteen dark fords. Then she arrived back at the Evanses.

But the pair were gone for the season. Much to her embarrassment, two young men—one a miner, the other a ranch hand—were "baching it" and looking after the stock. She had no choice but to remain, for the cold was so severe her boots and stockings were frozen on her feet. Suppressing her Victorian inhibitions, she and they decided to make the best of the situation. Be it said for the men, they showed the utmost chivalry and courtesy to her during her stay. When she insisted on doing her share of the work, they divided it, but gave her only the lightest chores. It was a pleasant, amusing time, but soon a shortage of rations—and regard for her reputation—made it advisable for Isabella to be on her way.

Mounting her pony Birdie, she rode to Longmouth in a furious east wind. It was a dangerous, exciting ride. Once the mare lost the trail completely. Then, arriving at the lake, they both fell through snow-covered ice into the water. It was a miracle they ever reached land again.

Isabella reached the hotel frostbitten, and so numb she could not dismount without aid. She was glad indeed to find Mr. Evans there with good news for her. Her money matters were again in order. But she had had enough of roughing it in the Rockies, and soon headed for home.

Isabella remained in England and Scotland for some years with her sister. They were busy writing years, for everyone at home and abroad was eager to read of Isabella's astonishing adventures, told in her lively style. They were eager to meet her, too, and always surprised at her petite feminine appearance. It seemed incredible that so frail a person could go to the most outlandish parts of the world, and return home —still a virtuous, soft-spoken Victorian lady.

The time came when Isabella felt the urge to go exploring again. In April, 1878, Isabella bid good-by to her sister and friends, and set out for Japan by way of Salt Lake City. There she was introduced to Mormon leaders, and stayed briefly in their homes. Then she went on to Yokohama where friends of her family, Sir Henry and Lady Parker, escorted her about. From there she went on to Tokyo, staying at the English legation and finding out all she could about the country.

"The great empire of Japan," she wrote her sister, "offers as much novelty, perhaps, as an excursion to another planet."

It was not Isabella's intent to be a mere tourist. Instead, she soon set out, off the beaten track, to visit a section never before penetrated by Europeans. Although friends at the legations worried greatly about Isabella's safety, she insisted on bringing with her only one attendant, a Japanese lad named Ito. Together they made a trek of 1200 miles through primitive regions, which she later recorded in her book, *Unbeaten Tracks in Japan.*

It was a fascinating journey, climaxed by her arrival at Boratori, in the northernmost island of Yezo, now Hokkaido. Here she lived for a brief time among the hairy Ainus, reputed to be the first inhabitants of Japan. They lived in a primitive state apart from the general populace, in a solitary mountain settlement reached only by traveling through a dark, silent forest where the main road at times dipped down into treacherous bogs. As Isabella struggled along this rude trail, her horse sank to his breast in one such bog. She shinnied up onto his neck then leaped over the horse to solid ground.

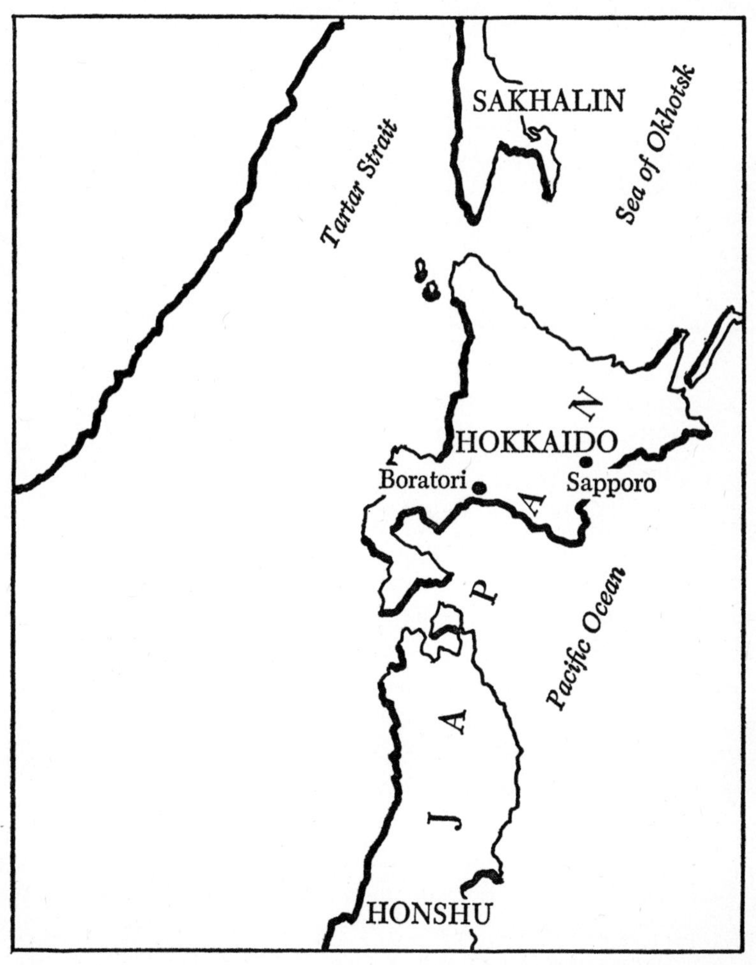

The northern part of Japan and the island of Hokkaido, where Isabella Bishop visited the Ainus.

The main group of Japanese looked on the Ainus as contemptuously as did Isabella's youthful servant. When Isabella mildly reproached him for his attitude, he looked at her in astonishment.

"But Missy, why treat the Ainus politely?" he puzzled. "They are mere dogs."

In the heart of the lonely Ainu land, she lived for three days and two nights in an Ainu hut, seeing and sharing the life of complete savages. With few exceptions, they did not regard her as an intruder. Most of them went on with their daily occupations as if she were not there, but they did insist on giving her a seat of honor, the guest seat—a raised platform at one end of the fire hole, with the skin of a black bear tossed over it.

As a savage drank a cup of saké, he saluted her first, then dipped a rod in the saké and made six libations to his god—an upright piece of wood, with fringe of shavings, propped up in the floor. Then he made other libations to the fire and drank.

Ten other men and women occupied the hut, sitting along each side of the fire hole, while the chief's wife cooked for them. Like many tribes she had visited, the women did most of the work, rising early to sew and weave, while the men slept, ate, or hunted.

She found them courteous, but primitive. In their own way, however, and despite the ferocious expressions of some of the men, Isabella concluded some of the children, at least, had beautiful faces and olive-tinted bodies. Until they were seven or eight, they went naked. Some were very hairy and even had fur on their backs; others were devoid of this covering.

To her surprise she found no polygamy here, even among the chiefs who were permitted to have three wives—provided each wife had her separate house. She learned the wives preferred monogamy; it meant a more peaceful existence.

Only one of their number spoke Japanese. He jabbered to Ito, and Ito interpreted for her.

One night, as she lay in her bunk, studying the faces of the savages made fiercer by the glow of log fire, she heard loud quarreling. With excited gestures, one of the men pointed toward her angrily. She thought her end was come. Soon the commotion ceased, and the men filed out of the hut, staring back at her hostilely, however. In the morning, she asked Ito what the fuss was about.

"It was nothing," he said. "One of the men was hot and wanted to take off his garment, but Shinondi, the chief's nephew, would not let him do it before a strange woman."

Washing was an unknown art to them, she soon discovered. When Isabella asked for water to bathe in, Shinondi handed her a lacquer bowl. As she washed her face and hands, he stared at her. She knew he was thinking that she was performing an act of worship to her own god.

Sleeping in clothes, lack of bathing, as well as enduring swarms of flies inside and outside the huts, soon made her tired of her stay. She left Boratori, and engaging an Ainu guide, "a formidable savage dressed in a coat of skins with his legs crossed over his horse's head," she explored the volcanic region near Volcano Bay. She wrote her sister: "My guide rode on the top of a pack-saddle . . . In one of the worst places, the Ainu's horse, in trying to scramble up a nearly breast-high and much-worn ledge, fell backwards, nearly overturning my horse, the stretcher poles which formed part of his pack striking me so hard that my ankle was severely cut and bled a good deal, and I was knocked out of the saddle. Ito's horse fell three times. Such are the divertissements of Yezo travel. Ah, but it was glorious! The views are most magnificent. This is really Paradise."

Paradise or not, she was glad to be on her way once more.

»»

From "Paradise" she went straight into a raging inferno; when her steamer reached Hong Kong, the whole city was suffering from the ravages of fire and dense smoke enveloped the harbor.

"It's no use going ashore," she was told. "The town's half burnt and burning still, and there's not a bed at any hotel for love or money!"

Nevertheless, Isabella went ashore, made copious notes about the desolate city, and even visited a friend of her father's, Bishop Burdon, at his unscathed palatial residence. There she was given letters of introduction to the governor of the Straits Settlement in Malacca, for she was anxious to explore in that vicinity on her way home.

When she arrived in Malacca, she spent some time as the guest of the British lieutenant-governor, Captain Shaw. At first, he was most unwilling that she travel into the interior, but when she insisted, he arranged for her to go to the native state of Sungei Ujong under protection of the British superintendent of police. This was enough of an encumbrance to Isabella but, in addition, he sent along his two daughters. To Isabella's dismay, they brought along trunks. She found them "totally unseasoned and inexperienced travelers, the preys of many terrors."

As for Isabella, she reveled in sights such as "the mangrove swamps where alligators were so common they ceased to be exciting" and "that enchanting wonder world of the jungle, with its orchids, ferns, lizards, flying foxes, and infinite variety of monkeys."

By the time they reached Sungei Ujong, the younger Miss Shaw was quite shaken up, and much in need of nursing at the British Residence. They remained there four days, then returned to Malacca, where they found they had been the talk of the small foreign world because of their daring.

Without the Misses Shaw, and glad to be on her own again,

Isabella went on to Klang and Selangor; while staying in the British Residence there the sultan's son, Rajah Moussa, paid a visit.

"He pretended to read the *Graphic*," wrote Isabella, "but instead, he studied me. Finally he asked me how many Japanese I had killed!"

With several Malays who knew no English, Isabella next penetrated into a region which had recently been the site of war, and was still regarded as dangerous and lawless. She went to the British Residence at Kwala Kangsa, but had no end of trouble with the elephant she rode. He was really a "wicked" one. She let him loose in the jungle, preferring to walk the remaining miles. Mr. Low, the resident, was away, but an Oriental butler received her ceremoniously, in spite of her mud-stained traveling gown.

Since her valise hadn't arrived, and she felt in no fit mood for company, she was embarrassed to find a table laid for three. She took her seat with some dismay. Then the butler led in a large ape and the Malay servant a small one. After that, a Sikh brought in a large retriever and tied him to Isabella's chair. This was all done with such solemnity that she didn't know whether to smile or be serious. The dinner proceeded with great dignity. "The apes ate their curry, chutney, pineapple, eggs, and bananas on porcelain plates," Isabella wrote to her sister, "and so did I. The chief difference was that, whereas I waited to be helped, the big ape was impolite enough occasionally to snatch something from a dish as the butler passed round the table, and that the small one soon migrated from his chair to the table, and sitting by my plate, helped himself daintily from it! What a grotesque dinner party! What a delightful one!"

Isabella left the Malay Peninsula late in February, 1879, on a steamer for Cairo. In Cairo she fulfilled a childhood dream, making a pilgrimage to Mount Sinai where she spent four days camping nearby. It proved to be a disillusioning experience, for Bedouins stole her caravan's water supply, and she and her Arab guides all but died of thirst. Back in Cairo, she came down with typhoid fever and nearly died. Weeks later, still ill, she decided a summer in Scotland was greatly preferable to the heat and dust of Cairo, and set out for her homeland, resolving to settle down and forget travel.

With her happy marriage to Doctor Bishop in 1881, and her comfortable life in Edinburgh, she only occasionally longed to set forth again for little-known regions of the globe. Since the doctor was far too busy at the Edinburgh Infirmary to take long vacations, Isabella now contented herself during the next several years with taking short trips with him to English seasides, or to the homes of their friends.

Then Doctor Bishop was stricken with fever contracted in the hospital ward; while he was recovering, Isabella came down again with her old spinal ailment.

The remainder of their five years together brought with it many bouts of illness for both of them. In between, they managed to find more contentment in each other's company than most hardy youthful couples.

"Queen Victoria is wrong," Isabella thought. "I will never leave Scotland and England again. My one desire now is to keep John with me. Or if he has to go, I want to go first."

But this was not to be. After a long illness, Doctor Bishop died peacefully in 1886. For a time, Isabella was too stricken to care about anything. Then she recovered sufficient health and will to throw herself into the study of medicine and nursing. Gradually, the desire to be on her way to far-off places returned. One day, the desire became too compelling to ignore.

In 1889, aged fifty-eight years old, Isabella Bishop set out for India. Arriving at Srinagar, she soon made arrangements for a hospital to be built there in memory of her husband. At Amritsar, she made similar arrangements for building a smaller hospital for women in memory of her sister, Henrietta.

On January 16, 1890, she started from Baghdad on a rugged journey beset with trial and many dangers. It took her more than 2500 miles, and embraced a circular tour through Persia, Kurdistan, Armenia, and Turkey up to Trebizond on the Black Sea.

Isabella finally arrived at the British legation at Tehran "caked with mud from head to foot, dripping, exhausted and nearly blind from fatigue," to find "every window lighted up, carriages dashing up with people in evening dress, and I invited to a large dinner party in my honor!"

In her book, *Journeys in Persia and Kurdistan*, Isabella described the splendors of Persian palaces she visited which made her realize for the first time "the fabled glories of the Arabian nights."

In Tehran, she found only pleasant experiences, but not so in Isfahan. For here the boys shouted at her, "Feringhi woman, a Nazarene woman," and called her vile names. Men laughed at her with fiendish oaths and howls, and she was spit upon. Her poor servant, Mahbound, was greatly distressed, but Isabella kept her head, and found haven at the English church Mission House in the Armenian suburb of Julfa.

The amir soon called to invite her to visit his wife. When he heard her tale of woe, he came to her rescue. That afternoon he sent her a beautiful horse and an escort of twelve cavalry soldiers. She was soon escorted past the city gate with "prancing and chatter, and no tongue wagged."

From Isfahan, Isabella made a hazardous journey into the mountainous region of Luristan, known as the Bakhtiari Country. It was inhabited chiefly by nomads, and in parts had never been explored by Europeans. She studied their cus-

Luristan, which is also called the Bakhtiari Country. Setting out from Isfahan, Mrs. Bishop took the route marked by the dotted line.

toms and beliefs, and nursed them. When a khan's brother was cured of fever, thanks to Isabella's care, she was offered a boy of five as a present. She politely declined this offer. Next the khan came to her tent and said:

"Though you are old, you can ride, and eat our food, and you love our people. Dwell among us till you are very old and be our Hakim and teach us the wisdom of the Feringhis."

But she did not stay. In spite of dangers, robberies, and other difficulties, she went on to Urmia, near the Turkish frontier.

Halting for a week on a plain of Gawar, in Turkish Kurdistan, she learned of appalling conditions in which Christian residents of the villages lived. There was much shooting and maltreatment of the women, and much robbery. Most of their houses were built underground, and their churches were like catacombs. She was impressed by the integrity and courage of these Gawar Christians, and from then on became a firm supporter of missionary work. Soon, too, she lay the case of these poor people before the grand vizier at Constantinople, and had the satisfaction of learning later that matters improved in the community.

She passed through solitary country and came to Kochaves, where she was a guest of the patriarch. He lived like a medieval baron in a stone dwelling with tower for refuge. He even had a jester.

Taking leave, she went on to the Armenian village of Khanjarah. Here she was discouraged from pitching her tents, as armed Kurds were always waiting to loot caravans. She lodged in a dark subterranean stable, but when she set out for Van, her caravan was attacked by Kurds. However, the robbers retired on seeing her Turkish escort. When she reached Van, the vice-consul was horrified she had taken such a dangerous route, but to Isabella, it added spice to her travels.

On December 12, 1890, she reached Trebizond, and embarked at Constantinople on her way to England. "It was journey's end, yet such is the magic charm of Asia," she wrote, "that I would willingly have turned back at that moment."

Isabella Bishop spent the next four years in Great Britain, where her reputation as traveler, writer, and lecturer made her welcome everywhere. She took lessons in photography, too, in order to improve her skill in this department. Soon she was elected a Fellow of the Royal Scottish Geographical Society, and of the Royal Geographical Society in England—the first woman to be given these honors.

But Isabella was not yet ready to settle down; in 1894, she set out again for the Far East, visiting Korea. She arrived at an important time in history, for the Chino-Japanese war had begun. On her first visit to Seoul, she saw "human heads hanging from tripod stands and lying on the ground in the throng of a business street." This visit was cut short by the arrival of the Japanese fleet and army. She left by steamer for Chefoo minus baggage and passport.

When she recovered these, she went on to Manchuria and China, and managed to reach there at a time when they were experiencing the worst floods they had known in years.

Not only that, but, when she journeyed up the Yangtze, she found that there was a new outbreak of feeling against the "foreign devils." On this trip, she was the recipient of a head blow from stones, and for months after suffered dizzy spells and headaches because of this.

She returned home, but not for long. In 1901, at the age of seventy, she set out alone for Morocco. The sea was so wild on her arrival at Mazagan that the captain insisted on her being lowered into the boat by ship's crane, in a coal basket. As she landed, officers cheered the white-haired old lady heartily.

This was quite enough to spur Isabella on to riding horseback astraddle for a thousand miles through Morocco, where she was entertained by Berber sheiks and khalifas in their castles. The sultan, who had never before received a European woman, gave her an interview, and she traveled as his guest in an expedition to the Atlas Range. In dreadful heat, she once had to ride for her life when pursued by armed Arabs, but in spite of these strenuous activities, she managed to return to Great Britain alive and in excellent spirits.

For a time after her homecoming, she was more active than ever. She wrote in her diary, "I had to go to Sheffield to give twenty lectures on China, New Japan, and Morocco, and thence, to the Bishop of Wakefields, to lecture in seven of the Yorkshire towns, and afterwards here, there and everywhere, having actually given forty-five lectures and addresses since October 17th. I have only slept once in my own bed for thirteen months."

Although she had looked forward to returning to China in the autumn of 1902, a swollen right arm which made writing difficult, and a weakness of her eyes, made her say to Sir Walter Hillier, "I had fully proposed to travel by the Jungting Lake to Kiver-chou, but it is very uncertain now, for I have been going down ever since October."

By December 23, she was confined to her bed in Edinburgh. Friends called on her often, and surrounded her with flowers and palms in pots. She especially loved the Christmas roses they brought, reminding her of her father's garden.

Whenever she was able, she "traveled at home" by looking out her bedroom window, which faced on flats in the rear, and waving to the tenants as they leaned out their windows and called to her.

She sent out her last New Year's cards in January, 1904, and her last entry in her diary was:

> "Upon a life I did not live,
> Upon a death I did not die—

Another's life—another's death—
I stake my whole eternity."

On October 7, 1904, the gallant Victorian lady, who had gone through countless hairbreadth escapes in foreign lands, died quietly in her bed. She was laid to rest in Dean Cemetery.

Friends who visited her shortly before her death said that her last words were:

"Oh what a shouting there will be!" This was an old family expression. It meant that after each long separation, there would be excited happy talking for members of the family when they met once more.

AUTHOR'S NOTE

One of the most challenging problems in organizing a book such as this—dependent as it is on geography—is comparing old maps with more recent ones in the effort to be as consistent as possible in spelling geographical names and locating places. For it must be clear to readers that maps are changing today with even greater rapidity than in the past. Especially is this true of continents in such constant turmoil as Africa and Asia.

Add to this the fact that seldom do two old maps, made by two different map makers of the same period, resemble each other in general appearance or in the spelling of names, and bear even less resemblance to maps we know, and you will have a faint idea of what an author of this type of book is up against.

Take, for example, the spellings of only a few of the African names mentioned in the book. Gondokoro, Africa, is not to be found on a modern map. But Gondokoro was well-known in the nineteenth century as a dismal trading station near the equator. It is mentioned in all records having to do with the explorers Alexine Tinnè and Florence Baker, and by a number of other explorers of their era. On old maps of Africa, and in frequent references made to this station by different explorers and historians of the period, it is variously spelled Gondokoro, Gondokorro, Gondoko, Gonkor, and other ways besides. It is not unusual for the same historian to spell it in several ways. So, too, I found Unjoro variously spelled as Unyoro, Bunjoro and Bunyoro; Niam-Niam as Nyam-Nyam and Niams-Niam; Cordafan as Kordafan and Cordafau. I could go on with instances of this sort, ad infinitum.

It is enough to say, however, that it came as a relief to me to find that *some* names I ran across in my research had only one alternative spelling! Khartoum was also spelled Khartoom; Lake Chad—Lake Tsad; Karuma—Karma, for example. But even in the case of Delia Akeley, who went to Africa alone in the nineteen twenties, I found variation in the spelling of such names as the seaport of Mambasa—Momboso, for instance, and names which, because of the later turn of events there, could no longer be located on maps.

Whenever possible, I have used the spellings of names and places in my stories favored by the Encyclopedia Britannica, or by authoritative recent maps. In instances where the names could only be checked in old sources, I used the spelling with which the majority of explorers or historians of the period seemed in some agreement.

Mignon Rittenhouse